HISTORY OF THE MARITIME CLOSED-CONE PINES, ALTA AND BAJA CALIFORNIA

History of the Maritime Closed-Cone Pines, Alta and Baja California

by Daniel I. Axelrod

UNIVERSITY OF CALIFORNIA PRESS
Berkeley • Los Angeles • London

UNIVERSITY OF CALIFORNIA PUBLICATIONS IN GEOLOGICAL SCIENCES

Editorial Board: D. I. Axelrod, W. B. N. Berry, R. L. Hay, M. A. Murphy,
J. W. Schopf, W. S. Wise, M. O. Woodburne, Chairman

Volume 120

Issue Date: June 1980

UNIVERSITY OF CALIFORNIA PRESS
BERKELEY AND LOS ANGELES
CALIFORNIA

UNIVERSITY OF CALIFORNIA PRESS, LTD.
LONDON, ENGLAND

ISBN: 0-520-09620-7
LIBRARY OF CONGRESS CATALOG CARD NUMBER: 80-51200

To NICHOLAS T. MIROV
In appreciation of his significant contributions
to our understanding of the pines of the world.

CONTENTS

HISTORY OF THE MARITIME CLOSED-CONE PINES, ALTA AND BAJA CALIFORNIA

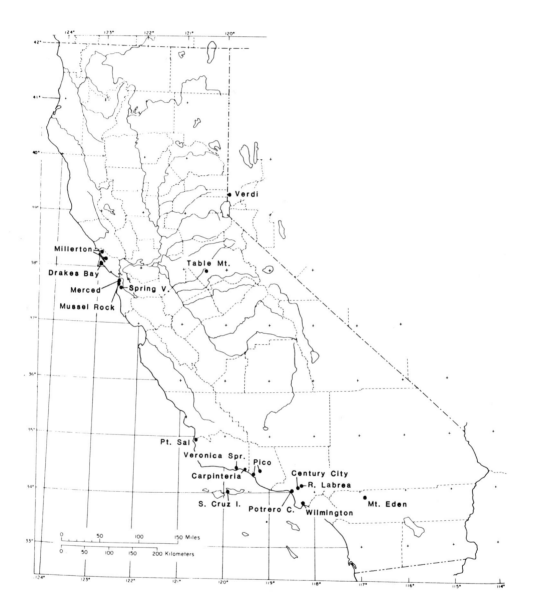

Fig. 1. California localities that have yielded significant fossil records of _Pinus_ subsect. Oocarpeae.

HISTORY OF THE MARITIME CLOSED-CONE PINES,

ALTA AND BAJA CALIFORNIA

ABSTRACT

Fossil Monterey pine cones 6-7 m.y. old are the size of the living Guadalupe Island and Monterey populations. Since cone size is a reliable taxonomic character in the group, it is inferred that the larger-coned California populations (Año Nuevo, Cambria) are younger, and that the smaller coned taxa on Guadalupe (var. binata) and Cedros (var. cedrosensis) islands probably are older. Development of larger cones with larger apophyses, greater asymmetry, and larger seeds in the California populations, may be correlated with the trend to increasing summer drought. By contrast, the Guadalupe and Cedros islands pines with small cones, reduced apophyses, more symmetry, and smaller seeds inhabit areas with summer rain, a feature typical of California into the Quaternary. Some Pleistocene radiata pines appear to represent extinct variants of this evolving chronocline.

The fossil Pinus masonii Dorf, recovered from rocks 9 m.y. old, is allied to P. "borealis" of the north coast. P. "borealis" appears to have hybridized with P. remorata Mason to produce the living P. muricata D. Don in late Wisconsinian or post-glacial time. P. muricata displaced the parental pines over most of their former range as summer drought increased after the last pluvial. The "muricata complex" thus includes "borealis", remorata, and the hybrid muricata.

Plate tectonic and floristic evidence suggest that Pinus subsect. Oocarpeae originated in western Mexico in pre-Miocene time. Two major evolutionary lines appear to have diverged from an ancestral oocarpa-like plexus. One with elliptic-elongate cones (attenuata, greggii, patula, pringleii) is largely interior and montane; the other, with ovate cones ("borealis", radiata, remorata) is chiefly in maritime California and insular Baja California. The Californian taxa were isolated gradually from their relatives on the Mexican mainland by spreading aridity over the developing Sonoran Desert region, opening of the Sea of Cortez, and northward displacement by the San Andreas and allied rifts following the Middle Miocene.

The notions that increased cone protection in California Oocarpeae, as provided by thicker or armed apophyses and greater cone asymmetry, resulted from coevolution with recent squirrels, or that fire had a role in their origin, are rejected. In the radiata line the trend to greater cone protection more probably reflects adaptation to increasing summer drought, since larger cones would produce larger seeds, which would be advantageous as drought stress increased. By contrast, cones of the equally ancient masonii-"borealis" and pretuberculata-attenuata lines were already stable 9-10 m.y. ago.

INTRODUCTION

The closed-cone pines of maritime Alta and Baja California include 3 species that now occupy discontinuous patches along the outer coast and on the southern islands (Critchfield and Little, 1966). These are Monterey pine (<u>Pinus</u> <u>radiata</u> D. Don), Bishop pine (<u>P</u>. <u>muricata</u> D. Don), and Island pine (<u>P</u>. <u>remorata</u> Mason), which most authorities believe represents a part of the variation of <u>P</u>. <u>muricata</u> (but see below). The history of these pines has been difficult to interpret because their fossil record has been limited chiefly to the Late Pleistocene. However, during the past decade a considerable body of new data that illuminates their earlier history has become available, so that its desirable to up-date an earlier report (Axelrod, 1967a). This new information includes older records that extend the age of the taxa down into older rocks, confirming their inferred antiquity. Also, new collections at old localities clarify the records of species that were based earlier on more fragmentary evidence. Furthermore, since the natural subsections of the genus have now been revised (Critchfield and Little, 1966; Little and Critchfield, 1969), it is possible to interpret the fossil records more realistically. Finally, during the past decade the rise of the new sub-

science of geology--plate tectonics--has provided evidence that demonstrates the shifting geographic setting of the California Oocarpeae during the Tertiary, and clarifies the historical affinity of the California
species with their nearest relatives in Mexico.

As a guide to the discussion, Figure 1 shows the California sites
that have yielded Neogene species of Pinus subsect. Oocarpeae that are
considered here, and Table 1 indicates their ages except for the Late
Pleistocene deposits, which are mostly in the range of 40,000 years or
less (see text).

MATERIALS FOR STUDY

The collections under study are composed primarily of pine cones.
Most of them are remarkably well preserved because they were rapidly
buried and subject to little or no damage during transport. Many are
unaltered and can be burned when dried, such as the Monterey pine cones
from Millerton, Drakes Bay, and Pt. Sal, and also the cones of "borealis"
(muricata of authors) from Pt. Sal. In some cases the cones still have
winged seeds that can be collected as the cones open after they are
dried. A different type of preservation is seen in the cones of radiata,
remorata, and "borealis" (= muricata) from Carpinteria, which are impreg-
nated with asphaltum. It is well established that cones provide a good
index to the nature of the species, and to the modern populations of
the taxa they represent. This is clear from the studies of P. radiata
conducted by Fielding (1953) and Forde (1964), of P. muricata by Duffield
(1951), and of P. contorta by Critchfield (1957). In their study of the
muricata-remorata problem, Linhart, Burr, and Conkle (1967) also relied
heavily on the nature of the cones.

In my collections at some of these rich sites, wood was encountered
in the form of stems and twigs, but fascicles of pine needles were not

TAXA AGE	radiata (lawsoniana)	"borealis" (masonii)	attenuata (pretuberculata)	remorata	MAMMAL AGES
QUATERNARY					RANCHOLABREAN
	Veronica Spr. Quarry				IRVINGTONIAN
PLIOCENE	⌐··Spring V. Lake			⌐··Century City	BLANCAN
	∣ Drakes Bay	∣ Merced		⌐··Potrero Cyn.	
		(2 locs.)			
	∣ Mussel Rock		∣ Verdi		
	∣ Mt. Eden		∣ Mt. Eden		HEMPHILLIAN
late		∣ Pico			
		(3 locs.)			
			∣ Table Mt.		CLARENDONIAN
MIOCENE					
		Wilmington			BARSTOVIAN
mid	[Santa Barbara]	(pollen)			
	see text				
					HEMINGFORDIAN
early					
					ARIKAREEAN

million years: 0, 5, 10, 15, 20, 25

seen.   On the other hand, Mason (1932, 1934), and Chaney and Mason

(1933) record the presence of abundant pine fascicles at two Pleistocene

sites.   At Carpinteria, Chaney and Mason (1933) considered the 2-needled

fascicles represented those of a large-coned Monterey pine.   However,

they did not discuss the possibility that the fascicles might represent

those of another common pine in the flora, the one identified as P.

muricata (= "borealis", see below).   It is a 2-needled pine, whereas

Monterey pine is chiefly 3-needled. Since the length of fascicles of

these pines is rather similar, the identity of the Carpinteria needles is

open to question.   Similarly, the 2-needled fascicles at Millerton were

referred to P. radiata by Mason (1934), yet the 2-needled P. "borealis"

is also in this deposit.   Furthermore, since needles are regularly lost

from a sheath, some 2-needled fascicles may have been 3-needled and could

just as well be referred to P. radiata.   As Mason notes (1932; also in

Chaney and Mason, 1933 p. 55), the number of needles in a radiata fasci-

cle is not constant, with some trees having as many as 30 percent of the

fascicles with only 2 needles.   Also, the Guadalupe variety binata

usually has 2 needles per fascicle, but those with 3 needles are not

uncommon (Mason, in Chaney and Mason, 1933, p. 55).   While cross-sections

of the needles might display consistent structural differences between

species, these were not examined in the earlier work, and fascicles are

not now available in the collections for study.

PINUS RADIATA D. Don

Comparison of the suites of complete, well preserved cones of the

fossil radiata alliance with large cone samples from the living popula-

tions provides the basis for this provisional evolutionary study of the

alliance.   As established by Fielding (1953) and Forde (1964), the pre-

sent radiata populations in California differ chiefly in cone size.

With increased cone size there are concurrent changes to larger apophyses, greater asymmetry, and larger seeds. As for cone size, Fielding (1953) gives mean figures for total cone length (geometric axis) in the California populations as: Monterey, 94.8 mm (3.74 in.); Ano Nuevo, 118.1 mm (4.66 in.); and Cambria, 143.2 mm (5.64 in.). Forde (1964) pointed out that since the cones are asymmetric, the geometric axis is a composite dimension determined partly by length of the curved axis, the terminal scales, and the thickness of the basal apophyses (Forde, 1964, fig. 4). By bisecting the cone longitudinally, she was able to study each of these variables separately. Her study shows that the population differences are proportionally similar to those recorded by Fielding (Forde, 1964, p. 465). Since the fossil cones can not be bisected without destroying them, the total cone length has been used for measurement. My cone collections from each of the living California populations give mean lengths similar to those presented by Fielding, though his Cambria measurements indicate a population of somewhat greater size (14.3 cm vs. 13.9 cm). This is not important to the present study, inasmuch as cones of this size are not now known from the fossil record.

With respect to using cone size, as well as related apophyses development and asymmetry, as a basis for evaluating the fossil record, it is emphasized that the modern samples used for comparison were collected throughout the living groves. Cones were gathered from trees on exposed slopes, in sheltered canyons, and around the perimeter of the groves as well. Older cones on the branches were also collected, so that those produced in less favorable years, as well as those from more favorable times, were also sampled. All cones were measured in the laboratory, not in the field. The collections of 350-odd cones from the 5 populations are thus believed to be representative of cone size in these populations,

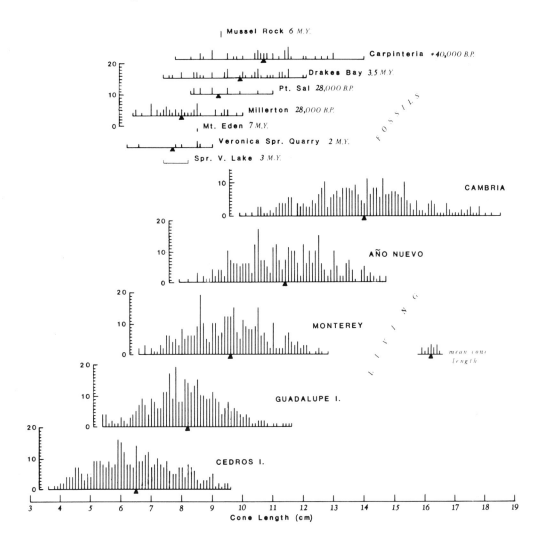

Fig. 2. Cone length in living and fossil populations of _Pinus radiata_ D. Don.

an opinion reinforced by the close agreement with the measurements made by Fielding (1953) and Forde (1964). The size of the cones of each of the living populations is illustrated in Figure 2, where the black pyramid under each population sample marks the mean cone size, and these are illustrated on Plate 1 for the 5 living populations.

Fossil Records

The Tertiary records of fossil Monterey pine, termed P. lawsoniana Axelrod, include an occurrence in the Miocene at Santa Barbara (Axelrod, 1967a). Two cones recovered during street work in the city were reported earlier as Pliocene (Mason, 1949, p. 357). I first examined these cones, which were then in the possession of Asbjorn P. Ousdal, in 1938. The cones are opalized, implying that they probably are from the Monterey Formation which underlies much of the city area. The cones are relatively small, more like the average from the population on Guadalupe Island or the larger cones from Cedros Island. Since it has not been possible after repeated efforts by several people to establish the whereabouts of this material, the record is shown in brackets in Table 1 to indicate this uncertainty.

This presumed antiquity for the radiata line of evolution is consistent with the occurrence of cones in the Mount Eden flora (Axelrod, 1937, 1967a) which is dated at about 7 m.y. by a large mammalian fauna. These cones are also small, more like those from Guadalupe Island than those of the present California populations. Monterey pine cones also occur in an old forest soil resting on the Franciscan diabase at Mussel Rock on the outer coast south of San Francisco (Lawson, 1915). Their position below the basal beds of the type marine Merced Formation indicates that they are not younger than about 6 m.y. (Glen, 1959). The cones are the size

of the present Monterey population.

Millerton

(Plates 2 and 3)

Mason (1932, 1934) assembled and studied more than 100 cones of

Monterey pine and associated needle fascicles (mostly in 2's) from 4

localities in the Upper Pleistocene Millerton Formation at Tomales Bay.

These have since been dated by radiocarbon at 29,050 $\pm$ 1,000 B.P. (Berger

and Thurber, 1966), and by Th^{230}/U^{234} as probably older than 50,000

years (Richards and Thurber, 1966). One of the localities is at

Millerton Pt., on the east shore of Tomales Bay at the east edge of the

San Andreas fault zone, and only 10 km northeast of the Pliocene Drakes

Bay fossils discussed below. The Millerton cones (Plates 2 and 3) are

much smaller than those from the Drakes Bay Formation (Plates 8-10), they

tend to be more symmetrical, and the apophyses are smaller and not so

swollen. On the basis of their size and the occurrence of numerous

2-needled fascicles, Mason concluded that the Millerton pine was most

nearly related to the present Monterey population, and that the living

dominantly 3-needled form at Monterey-Carmel probably originated more

recently.

One of the puzzling features of the Tomales collection is that the

only cone figured by Mason (1934, pl. 6, fig. 3) is 13 cm long, which is

slightly larger than cones in the Drakes Bay sample. However, Mason

(in Chaney and Mason, 1933, p. 55) emphasizes that the cones from the

Millerton localities rarely exceed 8 cm in length, indicating that they

average much smaller than the cones in the Drakes Bay sample (Plates

8-10). It has not been possible to solve this puzzle because the illu-

strated specimen has been lost for some years.   If it can be found,
examination of the sediment within the cone scales can demonstrate its
source.   For the present, it is believed that the figured cone (Mason,
1934, pl. 6, fig. 3) represents a specimen from Drakes Bay, not the
Millerton Formation.   A number of cones were known from this site at
that time according to Prof. Robert M. Bohart, who collected them and
presented them to Mason (personal communication, November 1976).

On the basis of cone length, the Millerton sample is much closer to
P. radiata var. binata Engelmann from Guadalupe Island than to P. radiata
at Monterey (Figs. 2-3).   However, the sample differs from binata in that
the apophyses on the fossil cones are more prominently swollen.   The
argument (Mason, 1932, 1934; Chaney and Mason, 1933) that the Millerton
cones are smaller than the norm of the present Monterey population
because they have dried and shrunk is not tenable for the entire collection.   Some of the cones recovered from the exposed cliffs above the tide
level have indeed shrunk, for they lie loose within a cavity in the rock.
But most of the cones at Millerton Pt. were recovered from the base of
the cliff in a wet blue-black silty mudstone below high tide level, and
also from the wet creekbed at Dillon Beach: at both sites the cones were
saturated and not shrunk.   Furthermore, it is readily demonstrable that
cones and other unaltered fossil plant material in museum collections
which have shrunk after 30-40 or more years can be restored to essentially their original size by submerging them in glycerine for a few
hours.   Also, additional cones recovered from the Millerton Formation,
which are the average size of those in the sample collected by Mason,
represent a pine that normally produced cones smaller than those of the
average Monterey sample.

Since the cones are small at all Millerton localities, and larger cones like the norm of the Monterey sample are not recorded, we appear to have evidence here for the presence of an alliance with small cones like the Guadalupe binata, but differing from it in having a greater number with more swollen apophyses. Furthermore, 2-needled fascicles are reportedly predominant in the Millerton sample (Mason, 1934), indicating another difference between the Millerton and any living population in California. These data do not support Mason's suggestion that the 3-needled, larger coned population at Monterey originated from the Millerton pine since 28,000 B.P. The Millerton population more probably represents an extinct alliance, one intermediate between the Guadalupe and Monterey populations.

With respect to the Millerton flora, it seems desirable to present some information that tends to modify an earlier interpretation of its paleoecology (Mason, 1934). It is recalled that the associated marine fauna has a number of warm-water mollusks that now live south of Pt. Concepćion (Mason, 1934; Campbell, 1974). This is consistent with evidence that the flora, dated at 29,000 to 50,000 years B.P., lived during an interglacial that preceded the Late Wisconsin drifts which commenced approximately 23,000 to 25,000 B.P. (see Flint, 1971, tables 20-A, 20-C, 21-D, 21-E). Since land areas were warmer--and the abundance of the 2-needled, small coned P. radiata in the flora implies this--there is no need to call on anomalous climatic conditions to explain the occurrence of colder north-coast plants associated with P. radiata and the warm water fauna at Tomales Bay (Mason, 1934).

The presence of Picea sitchensis, Arctostaphylos uva-ursi and Montia howellii at the Millerton Pt. locality, which suggest that a cold land climate was juxtaposed with a warm marine one, seems explicable by its setting in the 1.5 km-wide Tomales Bay rift valley into which streams drained from the east and west, and thence north to exit into the ocean near Dillon Beach. At Millerton Pt., the number and size of quartz diorite clasts in the conglomerates increase to the west. They are quite angular to subangular, and have not traveled far; they could only have come from Inverness Ridge to the west, across the present Tomales Bay. From east of the rift, Franciscan detritus composed of cobbles of chert, sandstone, and some serpentine was carried into the basin. These two sources account for the diverse composition of the cobbles in the con-glomerate at Millerton Pt. There the fossil plant bed is overlaid by strata that contain a marine fauna, indicating that the area subsided several feet following deposition of the plant bed, which is generally made up of blue-black mud of a swamp or lagoon-border at sea level. Since that time, Millerton Pt. has been uplifted fully 3-4 meters, exposing the marine interbeds.

The physical setting suggests that the rare taxa of cool requirements probably were transported to Millerton Pt. by streams draining the north easterly, cooler slopes above Inverness, possibly from Mt. Vision which is 3 km southwest and rises to 365 m. It or nearby parts of Inverness Ridge could have afforded cooler, more favorable sites than those at Millerton Point, where a small-coned Monterey pine population of southern affinity lived close to warm-water mollusks of present southern distribu-tion. The Millerton pine probably disappeared as a colder climate spread into the region during the Late Wisconsin (Tahoe-Tioga glacials). Final extermination may have resulted from the drier climate of the Xerother-mic, when the present discontinuous ranges of the surviving maritime pines were established (Axelrod, 1966a, p. 53).

Collection: U.C. Mus. Pal., Paleobot. ser.   Hypotype nos. 5762-
5770, homeotype nos. 5771-5786.

Carpinteria

The asphalt deposit at Carpinteria, which occurs in the elevated
stream terrace at the south edge of town (Putnam, 1942), has yielded
numerous cones of P. radiata.   Chaney and Mason (1933) considered that
they were most nearly allied to the present Cambria population.   In order
to assess their relations to other fossil and living populations, all
available complete cones in the collections at the Santa Barbara Museum
of Natural History and the Los Angeles County Museum of Natural History
were measured.   As shown in Figures 2 and 3, the Carpinteria cones are
intermediate in size between Ano Nuevo and Drakes Bay pine populations.
As for the Cambria population, it presently has no known fossil record,
and differs greatly from all others in its much larger cones.   The
reasons for this are suggested below in the discussion under Evolution.

Collections: Santa Barbara Museum of Natural History and Los
Angeles Co. Museum of Natural History.

Pt. Sal

(Plates 4 and 5)

The occurrence of cones of P. radiata in the Orcutt Formation, exposed in a deep (unnamed) canyon near Pt. Sal, has been noted earlier
(Axelrod, 1967a).   Although they are associated with numerous (over 100)
cones of P. "borealis" (see below), radiata cones are not common.   Only 5
partially complete ones were recovered initially, together with the
swollen apophyses of one other that had disintegrated upon exposure to
weathering.   On the basis of the relatively large size of those apophyses, it was suggested that the population might represent the large-coned

Cambria variant. However, a number of additional _radiata_ cones have now been recovered at the locality, and they clarify the affinity of the population that lived there.

There are 12 complete cones in the collection, and they are of intermediate size, as shown in Figures 2 and 3. The sample is admittedly small, yet it seems adequate to indicate that the fossils are more nearly allied to the Monterey than to the Cambria pine. Not only are the cones much smaller than the average for the Cambria norm, the apophyses are not as swollen or as large.

Collection: U.C. Mus. Pal., Paleobot. ser. Hypotype nos. 5787-5791, homeotype nos. 5792-5798.

Veronica Springs Quarry

(Plates 6 and 7)

During his long sojourn in Santa Barbara, Asbjorn P. Ousdal was an enthusiastic collector of the remains of fossil whales. Among the other items that he recovered from the marine rocks of the Santa Barbara area was an especially fine specimen of a cluster of 4 fossil Monterey pine cones. Fortunately, through the interest and efforts of Clifford F. Smith of the Santa Barbara Museum of Natural History, and the cooperation of Dale Whitney, the present owner of the Ousdal home, the fossil was located on display in the Masonic Temple, Santa Barbara. Members of that organization have generously presented it to the Museum of Natural History.

In addition, Scott Miller located 4 additional cones of fossil Monterey pine in the collections at the Santa Barbara Museum of Natural History. They were recovered from limy sandstones exposed at Veronica Springs Quarry, situated on the Mesa at Santa Barbara, 0.4 mile northeast of Veronica Springs. Scott Miller properly noted that these cones and the fossil cluster collected by Ousdal have a similar lithology. Together we have visited the site of the former quarry, and concur that this is most probably the locality from which Ousdal secured the cluster of cones. The tan to buff, well-cemented limy sandstone at the quarry, which was used for road metal chiefly, represents local cementation that resulted from an active spring. The cones are in the upper part of the Santa Barbara Formation, which is composed chiefly of poorly consolidated, buff to yellow brown, fine to coarse sandstone. A large megafossil marine fauna from the upper Santa Barbara Formation has _Pecten_ _caurinus_ as the most distinctive species (for other taxa, see Dibblee, 1966, p. 58). The age of the upper type Santa Barbara Formation is generally conceded to be Lower Pleistocene (see Dibblee, 1966), corresponding to the early Hallian Stage of the microfossil marine sequence and to the earliest part of the Irvingtonian Mammalian Stage, or possibly to the latest Blancan. The evidence indicates that the rocks from which the cones have been recovered are in the range of 1.5 to 2.0 m.y.

The cones are from 6.5 to 8.5 cm long, they vary fron nearly symmetrical to asymmetric, and the apophyses vary from poorly developed to moderately swollen. Since cone length in the modern _radiata_ populations overlaps to some degree (Fig. 2), a few specimens cannot be considered as definitive evidence for inferring affinity with any one population. Nonetheless, if we accept the probability that a small sample most likely falls near the average size of the cones in a fossil population, then it is clear that _in size_ the Veronica Springs cones are most nearly allied to _P._ _radiata_ var. _binata_ of Guadalupe Island. Supporting this conclusion is the fact that the fossil cones, like those of the var. _binata_, range from those with poorly developed apophyses to those that are sub-prominent. This implies that we probably are dealing with a population close to the living _binata_. The cones from Veronica Springs Quarry are also similar to the average cones of the Millerton sample of Late Pleistocene age (29,000 to 50,000 B.P.), and presumably represent the same taxon.

Collection: Santa Barbara Museum of Natural History, Hypotype nos. 183, 473, and 476-478.

Drakes Bay

(Plates 8-10)

The Late Pleistocene record of California species of closed-cone pines that form part of the subsection Oocarpeae is locally rich and remarkably well-preserved. This largely reflects their occurrence at sites of plant accumulation where their needles, cones, and other structures were quickly buried, thus removing them from various agents of destruction. Examples of preservation under such favorable conditions are provided by the rich records at Carpinteria (Chaney and Mason, 1933), Millerton Pt. (Mason, 1934), and near Pt. Sal (Axelrod, 1967a), all dated within the range of 28,000 to 40,000 years B.P. (Ferguson and Libby, 1964; Berger and Libby, 1966). They represent, respectively, floodplain-tarpit, estuarine-floodplain, and floodplain environments.

When we turn to the records of closed-cone pines from rocks of Early Pleistocene and greater age, we find that, although fossil cones occur at a number of localities, most are known from only one or two specimens, and these frequently are broken and eroded. Since the majority are in the marine section, they were deposited under circumstances (i.e., distance from shore, dispersal by currents, marine erosion, and other factors) in which cones would not only be rare, but in which the accumulation of a number of them at any one site would be highly unlikely. For this reason, the discovery of numerous unaltered and perfectly preserved fossil Monterey pine cones in a marine section which is here referred to as the "Merced Formation" is of considerable significance.

The occurrence was brought to my attention by Alan J. Galloway of the California Academy of Sciences, who discovered two cones in a sea-cliff while mapping the geology of the Pt. Reyes quadrangle. Several weeks later, another cone from the same locality was brought to my attention by Dr. Samuel P. Wells of the Museum of Paleontology, University of California, Berkeley, who found it while passing the site on the way to examine the remains of a fossil whale preserved in beds a few meters farther down the bay. This is the same locality that was discovered in the early thirties by the entomologist Robert M. Bohart, whose cone collection, which was presented to Mason, has been lost.

Geology. The Merced Formation on Pt. Reyes Peninsula is confined chiefly to the San Andreas fault zone near Bolinas, extending northward for about 11.5 km (7 mi.). Rocks of similar age reappear farther north, in the broad basin east of Bodega Bay, extending to the outskirts of Santa Rosa and Petaluma, where they interfinger with the Sonoma Volcanics (Dickerson, 1922; Weaver, 1949; Gealey, 1951; Travis, 1952). As noted by Galloway (1977), the rocks in the Bodega-Sonoma basin differ lithologically from the Merced Formation near Bolinas and from the Merced in its type area. The so-called Merced of the Bodega-Sonoma basin requires a new name, but until a type section is selected it seems best to refer to it as "Merced."

On Pt. Reyes Peninsula near Bolinas, the Merced is confined to the San Andreas trough. It consists of about 90-150 m (300-500 ft.) of soft sandstone and siltstone, and forms low, rounded hills (Galloway, 1977).

The lower part is chiefly soft siltstone and friable sandstone, with coarser beds in the upper part. The lower part evidently accumulated under shallow-water neritic conditions, probably in a sea less than 120 m (400 ft.) deep. Higher in the section, the beds indicate shallower water, and the top of the formation resembles a back-beach deposit (Galloway, 1977). The Merced silts contain large numbers of _Elphidella hannai_, an important foraminifera in the living fauna of San Francisco and Tomales bays. Galloway (1977, p. 361) lists the marine fossils in the Bolinas section, including species of echinoderms, bivalves, gastropods, and foraminifera. His review indicates that the Bolinas section corresponds to about the middle of the type Merced Formation exposed along Seven Mile Beach south of San Francisco, which is Late Pliocene. He also notes that the formation evidently was deposited in an inner bay, a relation suggested by Glen (1959) in his analysis of the type Merced fauna.

The plant-bearing sequence referred to here as the "Merced Formation" has not previously been recognized in the area west of Inverness Ridge on Pt. Reyes Peninsula for several reasons. First, the rocks in the area around Drakes Bay are poorly exposed, for the most part, being covered with thick grass and widespread, stabilized dunes. Outcrops of the younger rocks in the region have also been reduced by later uplift and erosion, and in some areas landslides obscure relationships. Apart from sea-cliff sections, good exposures are not present in the low terrain west of the Inverness Ridge.

The thin lens at the plant locality measures about 75 m long, but only about 1 m thickness is exposed. It rests on the Drakes Bay Formation and is covered by stabilized sand dunes that obscure it upslope. The fossil bed is a siltstone filled with numerous large (up to 4 cm) angular to subangular clasts of dacitic tuff in which biotite is rare. Galloway (1977, p. 31) was uncertain about the stratigraphic position of the cone-bearing bed. He indicated that it might be either a part of the Drakes Bay Formation or represent a younger unit, though he gave no reason for his indecision. I recently reexamined the cliff section in the company of Prof. Cordell Durrell.   As he notes, an unconformity separates the two units. First, there is a major structural difference. Two prominent sets of joints cut the Drakes Bay strata, but do not affect the immediately overlying plant bed.   Second, there is a notable change in lithology.   The siltstone of the plant-bearing bed has grains of quartz and feldspar in which are embedded numerous clasts of dacitic tuff, whereas the underlying Drakes Bay strata are chiefly hard, nodular mudstone and siltstone.   A third difference is suggested by a possible change in the attitude of the rocks, as exposed in the cliff section a short distance down the bay. The Drakes Bay beds dip 15-20° west, whereas the plant-bearing strata appear to be flat-lying. However, the attitude of the Drakes Bay strata is not well exposed at the plant locality, and since the dip of beds may change, the apparent difference in attitude is equivocal as compared with the evidence that indicates that the rock units differ lithologically and structurally.

As noted above, the clasts in the plant-bearing strata are a very fine-grained dacitic tuff with rare biotite.   Similar tuffs are widespread in the middle and upper parts of the Sonoma Volcanics (Gealey, 1951), and appear to be the source of the clasts in the plant-bearing section.   Dickerson (1922) records the occurrence of tuffaceous beds throughout the area of the "Merced Formation" in the Petaluma and Santa Rosa region, as do Gealey (1951) and Travis (1952). In his discussion of the relations between the strata of the "Merced Formation" and the Sonoma

Volcanics in the Healdsburg Quadrangle, Gealey (1951) emphasizes that the most important volcanic constituent of the Sonoma rocks is pumice tuff of dacitic composition. The tuffs, from 120 to 150 m (400-500 ft.) thick, overlie the lower basalt flows, and another tuff unit occurs at higher levels. The tuffs are light gray to white and generally massive, and pumice fragments 0.5 to 2 in. in diameter are abundant at many horizons. In addition to the tuff bodies, Gealey (1951) emphasizes that all Sonoma sedimentary rocks are tuffaceous.

The Sonoma interfingers with the "Merced Formation" at Wilson Grove, 5 km (3 mi.) southwest of Windsor, where there is a large associated molluscan fauna (Weaver, 1949, p. 95). The fossiliferous "Merced" strata conformably overlie 60 m (200 ft.) of Sonoma tuff that forms a marine wedge in the Sonoma Volcanics. In the adjoining Sebastopol quadrangle to the south, Travis (1952) notes there is a similar interfingering of these rock units. Farther east, the "Merced" consists of medium-grained sand-stone that interfingers with freshwater sediments and Sonoma volcanic rocks, including beds of tuff breccia, tuff, and conglomerate composed of fine tuffaceous material and rounded pebbles of pumice tuff.

I have visited these areas and collected tuffs from several sites that seem inseparable from the tuff clasts in the plant beds. The evidence suggests that the plant bed is a remnant of the "Merced Forma-tion" that formerly had a more continuous distribution prior to uplift and erosion. This is consistent with the occurrence in the marine Merced Formation of thin (1 to 3 cm) lenses of reworked white- to-gray, fine tuffaceous sandstone and siltstone beds that appear to be dacitic in composition. Several of them are exposed in road cuts along State Highway 1 north of Bolinas.

The Sonoma tuff at Petrified Forest about 5 miles east of Santa Rosa has been dated at 3.5 m.y. (Evernden and James, 1964). The tuff is similar to those abundant in the "Merced Formation" in the Bodega basin west of Santa Rosa and Petaluma, which contains the molluscan fauna that is considered equivalent in time to the middle of the type Merced Formation (Weaver, 1949; Glen, 1959). The data indicate that the fossils are Early Blancan in terms of the mammalian faunal chronology (Evernden et al., 1964; Durham, Jahns, and Savage, 1954), and Late Wheelerian in the microfossil sequence (Bandy and Ingle, 1970). Fossil floras from the several localities in the Santa Rosa region and near Petaluma, in the Sonoma sediments and in the "Merced," have also been considered Late Pliocene (Dorf, 1930; Axelrod, 1944, 1950).

Mode of Occurrence. The fossil cones and associated twigs and small branches crop out in a low sea-cliff where they are exposed by wave erosion that undercuts the bank, promotes slumping and caving, and thus uncovers new material. The site has been visited on 9 occasions over a period of 12 years to collect whatever new material has become available. Most of the cones are complete. The broken ones appear for the most part to be the result of weathering in the cliff and slumping of the enclosing shale, which breaks the cones that are soft and pliable, owing to their twice-daily immersion in sea water. The sample of 40-odd cones now available seems sufficiently large to be considered representative of the species.

The cones and associated plant debris occur in a submarine mudflow-breccia. As exposed in the sea-cliff, the base of the mudflow is irregular for it has eroded broad, concave channels into the underlying mudstone of the Drakes Bay Formation. The cones are concentrated near the middle of the mudflow, in its thickest part where they probably were afforded greater bouyancy for transport. Since the cones and stems are unaltered, they must have been buried immediately and thus removed from fungi, bacteria, scavengers, and other agents of destruction. When dried out, they can be burned with no difficulty. A few of the cones are partially flattened by compaction of the sediments that accumulated later.

The concentration of numerous complete, unaltered cones in a perfect state of preservation in a marine deposit requires explanation.   Since the San Andreas fault zone is situated only 10 km east of the locality, where it occupies the narrow trough of Tomales Bay, the possibility arises that the submarine mudflow in which the cones occur may have been triggered by a major earthquake and its accompanying aftershocks. A similar mechanism was invoked by Woodring, Bramlette, and Kew (1946, p. 32) to explain the occurrence of breccia lenses of Catalina Schist and Altamira Shale in the Altamira Shale Member of the Monterey Formation in the Palos Verdes Hills.   In an attempt to decide on the possibility of such an explanation, as contrasted with a more "normal" mode of accumulation, the modern groves near Ano Nuevo Pt., Monterey-Carmel, and Cambria were examined. Complete cones were found under many of the trees in all of the groves. At Cambria, 5 different groups of perfect cones ranging from 5 to 13 in each group were found lying on the broad dry bed of Santa Rosa Creek in June 1977. Each cluster was under a different tree and ready for water-transport to the coast, situated only 1 km distant. Clearly, at times of flood the cones could easily be carried into the lagoon and thence swept seaward. Nonetheless, the number of cones available for transport could be augmented by the violent shaking of a major quake. The quake may also have triggered the mudflow breccia that carried the cones into deeper water, though instability of the sediment on a steep slope inshore may have released the material.

In an inshore deposit bordered by high terrain, one might expect coarse detritus such as sand and gravel, but none is present at the locality. This implies that the cones were transported into quiet water, largely beyond the zone of coarse sand and gravel deposition. They moved in a submarine mudflow that scoured the bottom and ripped up sections of the accumulated siltstone, carrying them together with the associated plant debris into deeper water. The bordering land area probably was low and under a regime conducive to deep weathering. The shoreline may have been at the site of the present Inverness Ridge, which must have been quite low at that time. The area was situated west of the San Andreas fault, on which there has been continuing movement since the Miocene. Judging from known displacement on the rift (e.g., Smith, 1977; Silver and Normark, 1978; Crowell, 1962, 1975; Ehlert and Ehlig, 1977; Kovach and Nur, 1973; Matthews, 1976), the area probably was opposite San Francisco, about 40 km (25 mi.) south-southeast.

The large suite of cones from the "Merced Formation" at Drakes Bay has been compared with those of the living populations in California and Baja California (Fig. 2). In length, the Drakes Bay cones are more nearly like those of the present Monterey population than any other. The collection further establishes the antiquity of the radiata alliance which has previously been reported from the Mt. Eden flora (7 m.y.) and from the old forest soil that underlies the basal type Merced Formation which is not less than 6 m.y. It seems probable that in terms of cone size, as well as shape, apophyses development, and asymmetry, the P. lawsoniana populations changed only gradually during the past 7 m.y.

Collection: U.C. Mus. Pal., Paleobot. ser., Hypotype nos. 5799-5806,

homeotype nos. 5807-5838.

Evolution

Population relations and age

As for the evolution of the different Monterey pine populations,

there is now (after 80-odd years!) only limited evidence regarding the

alliance. To interpret their history it is essential to keep in mind the

nature of the different modern populations. As established by Fielding

(1953) and Forde (1964), those at Monterey-Carmel, Año Nuevo-Swanton, and

Cambria differ importantly in cone length. The data presented here for

the variety binata from Guadalupe Island, and the variety cedrosensis[1]

from Cedros Island, fit readily into their results (Fig. 2). Using cone

length as a taxonomic character, a quantitative analysis of the living

and fossil populations indicates relationships that are relatively

well-defined. A statistical test[2] of the difference between means of

each pair of population sample, both living and fossil, was kindly per-

formed by Robert Robichaux, and the results are summarized in Figure 3.

The numbers beneath each population represent the mean, standard devi-

ation, and sample size, respectively, for the data in Figure 2. All

of the populations unconnected by solid lines are statistically signifi-

cantly different (α 0.05).

Figure 3 shows that in terms of cone length the fossil Veronica

Springs and Millerton samples are most nearly related to the Guadalupe

Island var. binata, while the fossil Pt. Sal and Drakes Bay populations

show greatest affinity with the living stands at Monterey-Carmel. The

fossil Carpinteria sample is intermediate between the Monterey and Año

Nuevo populations. Although its mean cone length more nearly approaches

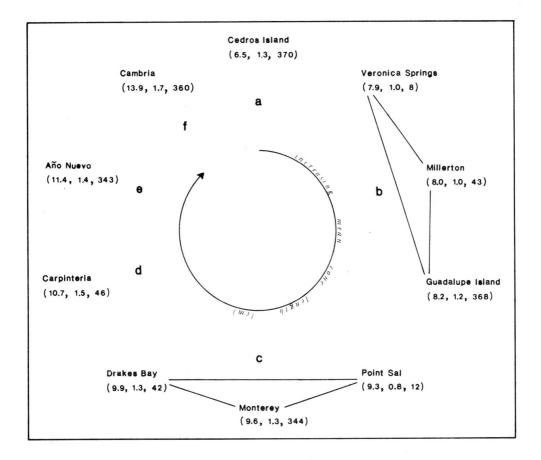

Fig. 3.   Quantitative relationships of cone length in living and fossil populations of <u>Pinus</u> <u>radiata</u> D. Don. (data from Fig. 2). Numbers under each population sample represent, left to right, the mean, standard deviation, and sample size.

the latter than the former, it is still statistically significantly different from both. As judged from the available record, the large-coned Cambria and the small-coned Cedros Island populations are not related to any known fossil populations, and are very distinct from all other living populations.

Viewed in this light, we see that in terms of population norm the large fossil sample from Drakes Bay is intermediate to the Carpinteria-Cambria and the Guadalupe-Cedros samples. This implies that the Guadalupe-Cedros populations are older than 9 m.y. and that the Año Nuevo-Cambria are younger. In the same way, the Monterey population is so similar to the Drakes Bay that it probably has derived from it, and may represent no more than a bradytelic population of essentially similar age. On the other hand, the small cones of the living Guadalupe Island var. binata, which are the size of the fossil Mt. Eden, Crystal Springs, Millerton, and Veronica Springs samples, suggest that the Guadalupe may be more ancient than any of the living California populations. The available data imply that the small-coned Cedros Island var. cedrosensis probably is the oldest of the radiata populations, and that the large-coned Cambria population is the youngest.

These inferences, which imply a general trend toward increased cone size and greater asymmetry in the Pinus radiata line of evolution, are supported by several lines of evidence. The smallest are most nearly like the presumed ancestral form of the Oocarpae which probably was similar to the modern P. oocarpa of Mexico (Critchfield, 1967). Furthermore, the fact that the populations with the smallest cones are in areas with summer rain implies that they may be older, because that condition was prevalent in California and northern Baja California during the later Tertiary, and characterizes the area of oocarpa and its relatives in

Mexico today. Also, the oldest cones (Mt. Eden, Mussel Rock) are rela-

tively small, as are the opalized cones presumed to be from the Monterey

Formation at Santa Barbara. Figure 2 shows that the cones from younger

rocks (Drakes Bay, Carpinteria) are larger than those from the older

horizons. As shown also in Figure 2, the variation in size of the dif-

ferent samples falls into similar modes which imply that the largest-

coned taxa (Año Nuevo, Cambria), which do not have a known fossil record,

may have originated more recently. Although there may have been a rever-

sal of trend or a reticulate pattern in the evolution of these popula-

tions, the most parsimonious explanation for the data now in hand is that

the trend has been linear.

While cone length gives a clue to the relations of the fossil to

modern radiata populations, there is another factor that must be consid-

ered. This is the nature of the apophyses on the cone scales, a feature

that is not readily measurable. Nonetheless, comparison of the fossil

populations with the modern ones most nearly like them in terms of both

cone and apophyses size does reveal significant features, as indicated in

Figure 4. The curves on each axis imply a range of variation for the

modern populations, and the position of the fossils in the squares indi-

cates approximately their relations to the living populations. Also

included for comparison are cones from several sites where the species

is known from only one or two cones. It is evident that some of the

fossils, whether the populations represented by numerous cones, or

those by a few, appear to differ from modern variants of Monterey pine.

They therefore appear to be extinct populations (or variants). From the

records at hand, it appears that cone size in fossil Monterey pine

populations has shifted in time from small to large, that in California

populations the apophyses have increased in size, and that the cones have

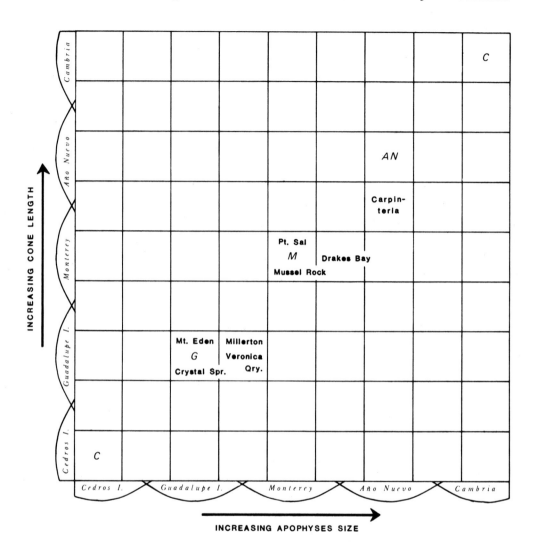

Fig. 4. Comparisons of cone length and relative apophyses size in living and fossil populations of <u>Pinus</u> <u>radiata</u> D. Don. The comparison implies that some fossil populations are extinct.

become more asymmetrical. This further supports the inference of others regarding the general trend of cone evolution (Mason, 1932; Fielding, 1953; Forde, 1964).

The data suggest the recent fragmentation of formerly more wide-spread and variable populations, with local extinctions for the Carpin-teria, Veronica Springs, and Millerton samples. In any event, it seems clear that bradytely has been a dominant mode in the alliance. The general picture that emerges from the limited evidence now in hand recalls the successive deployment of a taxon into a series of subzones (Simpson, 1953, fig. 50), with the survival of some of the linking modes. Thus, we appear to have evidence for a slow shift in the average charac-ters over a period of many million years, for the line was certainly established long before the oldest known records. The significant point is that the presumed oldest (Cedros) and youngest (Cambria) forms have persisted (Fig. 5).

The relations that suggest a general trend to larger cones, thicker apophyses, and greater asymmetry imply that the Cedros and Guadalupe pines are older than the Drakes Bay, and that the Ano Nuevo and Cambria are younger. As noted above, this has the merit of relating the presumed older, smallest-coned taxon to the Mexican *oocarpa* which it generally resembles, and which may well represent an alliance close to the ances-tral form of the group. In addition, we can account for the existence of variable populations in the past, some of which are no longer living (Millerton, Veronica Springs, Carpinteria). Clearly, additional fossil data are needed to choose between this or other alternatives that may have been followed during the history of Monterey pines.

The living P. radiata populations do not represent as a cline. Al-though those in California are not in geographic order in terms of cone

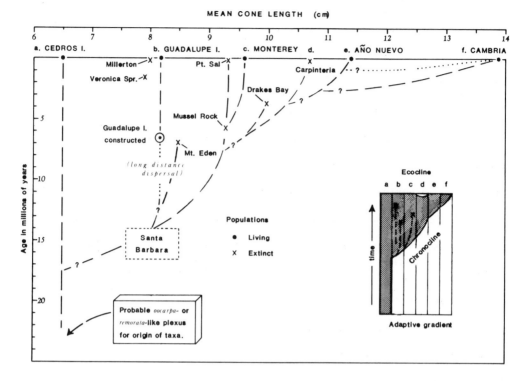

Fig. 5. Inferred relationships of fossil populations allied to <u>Pinus</u> <u>radiata</u> D. Don (from data in Figs. 2 and 3). The pattern suggests a chronocline (inset), as depicted by Simpson (1953, fig. 50).

size (the trend northward from Cambria to Monterey to Año Nuevo is from

large to small to medium size), this might be explained by population

shifts during the fluctuating climates of the Late Pleistocene. However,

such a simple explanation is not supported by the fossil record.   It

shows that in the Late Pleistocene a Monterey-like population lived at

Pt. Sal, situated south of the present California groves.   Furthermore,

the rich Millerton record reveals a 2-needled, small-coned pine with

relatively prominent apophyses, a pine more like the Guadalupe Island

var. binata than any other now living, although occasional trees in the

Monterey area may produce cones not unlike the fossils.   Furthermore, the

Millerton record, dated at older than 29,000 B.P., is well north of

any living California populations.   Also, the southern Carpinteria pine

is intermediate between the Monterey and the Año Nuevo population, which

is at present the most northerly stand.   Such records imply that, rather

than a simple disrupted cline of Late Pleistocene age, the fossil groves

more probably represent variable populations from which the living were

derived.

A problem in distribution

The inference that the 2-needled, small coned P. radiata var.

cedrosensis is the oldest in the radiata line seems consistent with the

nature of insular floras in general, and with the history of the Califor-

nian islands in particular.   In brief, the Cedros Island taxon may well

be the descendant of an ancient (or ancestral) mainland alliance that

persisted in a favorable site as the island was isolated under mild

maritime climate during the Pliocene.   It is recalled that several

of the endemics that typify the islands off southern California,

(e.g., Laurocerasus (Prunus) lyonii; Lyonothamnus floribundus, and L.

Table 2.　Wood plants on Cedros Island that occur also on the nearby mainland or on Californian islands to the north (Eastwood, 1929a; also Reid Moran, personal communication, 1978)

Cedros Island	Coastal Northern Baja California	S. San Pedro Martir (lower)	Californian Islands	Coastal So. California
Pinus radiata var. cedrosensis	....	....	P. radiata on San Miguel I. in Late Pleistocene (Johnson, 1977)	P. radiata at R. La Brea and Carpinteria in Pleistocene
Juniperus cerroensis	....	(californica)	....	(californica)
Ephedra aspera	sp.	sp.		
Adenostema fasciculatum	x	x	x	x
Baccharis sarothroides	x	x	x	x
Celtis reticulata		x	....	....
Ceanothus verrucosus	x	x	....	x
Cneoridium dumosum[a]	x	x	....	x
Condalia parryi var. microphylla	....	x	....	....
Euphorbia misera	x	x	x	x[b]
Galvesia juncea	x		x	
Garrya veatchii	x	x	x	x
Happlopappus propinquis	x	x	....	x
Heteromeles arbutifolia	x	x	(var. macrocarpa)	x
Isomeris arborea	x	x	x	x
Lonicera subspicata var. denudata	x	x	....	x[b]
Lycium brevipes	x	x	x	....
Malosma laurina	x	x	x	x
Quercus cedrosensis	x	x	....	....
Rhamnus insula	x	x	....	....
Rhus integrifolia	x	x	x	x
Rhus lentii	(Viscaino Peninsula)	....	....	....
Ribes viburnifolium	x	....	Catalina I. only	....
Simmondsia chinensis	x	x	....	x[b]
Viscainoa geniculata	x	x	....	x[b]
Xylococcus bicolor	x	x	x	x[b]
Xylonagra arborea	(coast-central Baja Calif.)	....	....	....

a　Apparently not previously reported.
b　In the Diegan region.

asplenifolius; Pinus remorata; Quercus tomentella) have Tertiary records

on the mainland.   Many of the woody taxa on Cedros Island evidently have

had a comparable history, to judge from their systematic affinities and

from their distribution as well.   As listed in Table 2, a number of them

occur in insular southern California, or in northern Baja California, and

some also have fossil records on the mainland.   In addition, there are

unique endemics on the Cedros, notably Xylonagra (Onograceae) and Rhus

lentii that have only relictual, isolated occurrences on the nearby main-

land.   Clearly, they are members of a distinctive vegetation that repre-

sents a coastal segregate of the Madro-Tertiary woodland that was dis-

rupted by spreading aridity (Axelrod, 1958, 1979).   An alternate explana-

tion, that the var. cedrosensis is relatively young, and developed small

cones in response to the increasingly drier climate that culminated in

desert conditions, runs counter to the fossil record itself.   Relatively

small cones appear in the record first (Santa Barbara, Mt. Eden), large

cones later.   Also, adaptation to increasing aridity implies that the

"successful" taxon might be expected to have a wider distribution than it

does.   Until definitive, contrary evidence is found, it is regarded as a

relict taxon.

How can we account for the Guadalupe population that occurs on an

oceanic island built up from the deep ocean floor 7 m.y. ago?   The

Guadalupe trees are larger than those on Cedros, and the Guadalupe cones

are consistently larger (Fig. 2).   One possibility visualizes establish-

ment of a Cedros pine on Guadalupe Island and its gradual evolution into

a larger-coned population, in response to the moister climate there.   On

the other hand, the record shows that cones the size of the Guadalupe

var. binata occur at Veronica Springs Quarry (2 m.y.) and in the Mount

Eden flora (7 m.y.).   Inasmuch as they differ from binata chiefly in

Table 3. Woody plants on Guadalupe Island that occur also on the nearby mainland or on
Californian Islands (Eastwood, 1929b; also Reid Moran, personal communication, 1978)

Guadalupe Island	Coastal Northern Baja California	S. San Pedro Martir (lower)	Californian Islands	Coastal So. California
Pinus radiata v. binata	....	....	P. radiata on San Miguel I. in Pleistocene (Johnson, 1977)	P. radiata at R. La Brea and Carpinteria in Pleistocene
Cupressus guadalupensis	*(forbesii)	*(forbesii)	....	*(forbesii)
Juniperus californica	....	x	....	x
Brahea (Erythea) edulis	*(B. armata N. to San Simon, 30°30')	....	....	....
Arctostaphylos sp.	spp.	spp.	spp.	spp.
Ceanothus crassifolius planus	....	....	....	....
Ceanothus insularis	....	....	x	*(megacarpus)
Crossosoma californicum			x	(near Pt. Vicente)
Lavatera occidentalis	(Coronado I.)	....	*(assurgentiflora)	....
Lycium californicum	x	x	x	x
Malosma laurina	x	x	x	x
Quercus tomentella	....	....	x	....
Rhamnus pirifolia	....	....	x	....
Rhus integrifolia	x	x	x	x

* (Allied species indicated in parenthesis)

having slightly larger apophyses, they probably were derived from a binata-type pine. Since they lived under a summer-wet climate, this suggests that the Guadalupe pine has been confined to similar areas throughout its history. On this basis, it probably invaded the island from the adjacent mainland at an early date, prior to the spread of the Sonoran Desert (Axelrod, 1979). That binata probably has some antiquity is implied also by its associates. As listed in Table 3, many of them occur in woodland vegetation on the mainland to the north in Baja California, or on the California islands, or in cismontane California.[3/] In addition, Guadalupe was the home of the notable endemic Hesperalaea, an evergreen monotypic sclerophyllous small tree in the Oleaceae that is now extinct. The notion that Guadalupe P. radiata var. binata invaded the island from the nearby mainland during a moister phase of the Quaternary, disappearing from the mainland as desert climate spread widely there, seems less likely. Its long exposure to drought on the peninsula presumably would have resulted in the development of larger apophyses and seeds (see Coevolution and Cone Morphology).

As for the disruption of the range of former stands of P. radiata, evidence suggests that the groves were confined to their present areas by spreading drought, and chiefly during the Xerothermic (Axelrod, 1967a). The elimination of populations during the later Quaternary has especially accentuated the differences that now exist between the surviving populations, as the Pt. Sal, Carpinteria, and Millerton records indicate. Clearly, the discovery of fossil pines at sites in Baja California, as well as elsewhere along the coastal strip in southern California, may clarify these and other problems still posed by the history of P. radiata.

Systematic treatment

The relations of the suites of fossil cones to one another, and to modern populations, raise a difficult taxonomic problem. In view of the limited material representing the Pinus radiata chronocline after 80-odd years of collecting, is it desirable or meaningful to formally name these populations? Considered individually, the suites of cones from Millerton and Drakes Bay, situated only 10 km apart, certainly warrant description. However, the data in Figure 2 make it clear that the description of any fossil population must be arbitrary, because the links between any designated taxa are indefinite and blurred, and additional fossil finds will certainly modify our views of them. For these reasons, it seems wiser to refer to them by locality name as the Millerton, Drakes Bay or Veronica Springs pines (or taxa), much as we refer to the living populations at Monterey, Año Nuevo Pt., or Cambria with reasonable clarity. In this manner we can accommodate new finds with no difficulty, and as additional material accumulates it will be possible later to place them in a more natural classification. Those that are older than Pleistocene are referred arbitrarily to P. lawsoniana Axelrod, which indicates their antiquity and emphasizes that they lived under very different climates.

PINUS MURICATA D. Don

(Plate 11)

The taxonomic problems raised by P. muricata and P. remorata of insular and maritime California and northern Baja California have been discussed for some time (Mason, 1930, 1932; Howell, 1941; Duffield, 1951; Fielding, 1953; Linhart, Burr, and Conkle, 1967; Critchfield, 1967; Critchfield and Little, 1966). There is general agreement that specimens are difficult to place taxonomically, because in population samples there is a continuous series from remorata-type cones (symmetrically ovate, smooth apophyses) to those typical of muricata (strongly asymmetrical, prominently hooked apophyses). The wide range of variation in muricata populations is nicely illustrated by Duffield (1951) and by Linhart, Burr, and Conkle (1967), and is also shown here on Plate 11, which is a sample of cones from the muricata grove adjacent to State Highway 1 on the crest of Purisima Ridge 10 km north of Lompoc. The consensus has been that remorata is not a valid species, but a name given to a particular cone type at one extreme of the variation of muricata; hence it does not deserve specific recognition.

In his detailed study of P. muricata throughout its area of distribution, Duffield (1951) distinguished 3 variants which he informally named. Var. "typica" occurs on the central and south coast, with the type area in the Pecho Hills west of San Luis Obispo, the locality for the initial description of P. muricata. The cones of "typica" are variable in shape and armament. They range from ovate-elliptic, with nearly smooth cone scales, to those with prominently hooked apophyses. The variety "borealis," inhabiting the coast from Sonoma County northward, is represented by trees of larger stature; the cones are less serotinous, and they are typically ovate with prominently hooked apophyses. Two distinct populations have been recognized in this area (Critchfield, 1972); the more northerly one typically has a dark blue-green aspect related to stomatal shape and waxiness, and coincident with one of the three chemical races (mostly alpha-pinene). This race is continuous with the green-foliaged 3-carene race on the Sonoma County coast, where the two races intermingle and hybridize. As for remorata, described by Mason (1930), it has symmetrical cones and the scales are thin and plane. It is confined chiefly to Santa Cruz and Santa Rosa islands, but has mainland occurrences at Pine Canyon near Lompoc and also in the lower part of Cañon de los Piñitos, southwest of San Vicente, Baja California. Trees are a lighter green, branches stand nearly normal to the trunk, the cones are normal to the stems, and the stems are brittle as compared with those of the more pliant "borealis" and "typica" variants.

Duffield records detailed data regarding the differences among these 3 variants. He notes differences in the needles, which are heavier in the northern population as judged from dry weight analyses. Also the mean resin canal number of remorata is 5.7 per needle, which is intermediate between the southern San Vicente var. "typica," with a mean of 7.0, and the Purisima population of "typica," with mean of 4.1. The latter sample mean has associated with it the highest coefficient of variation in the entire series, implying segregation that reveals past or continuing hybridization, according to Duffield. In addition, Mirov (in Duffield) reports that the optical rotation of the crude terpenes shows that remorata is very different from the northern "borealis." Duffield also records differences in bark fissure width and depth, with 8 mm and 4 mm respectively for remorata but much higher for "borealis" and "typica." Furthermore, Duffield notes that cones of the northern "borealis," adapted to a more humid climate and more dependable precipitation, are less serotinous. In late summer many trees in the northern stands have cones of the preceding year open, whereas in the south they are closed. Critchfield (personal communication, 1977) has also observed that remorata cones mature earlier than "typica" or "borealis" from the more northern localities, which is consistent with its warmer, drier requirements.

I have noted that the 3 varieties of _muricata_ have different ecologic preferences.   _Remorata_ occurs on the driest sites.   It is on the elevated well-drained conglomeratic terrace in Pine Canyon north of Lompoc, whereas "_typica_" occurs there, but below the terrace on dipping diatomite, which is sufficiently moist so that at the end of a long summer yellowjackets are attracted to it.   At Canon de los Pinitos, _remorata_ is in the lower part of the canyon, which is entrenched into the elevated marine terrace at an elevation of about 300 ft.   The form "_typica_" is also in the area, but reaches best development upstream on the north-facing, cooler slopes of a high ridge that reaches up to 1,500 feet.   In that area the shrubby associates of var. "_typica_" are more mesic, and also include _Cupressus_.

Finally, note must be made of the significant observation by Duffield (1951, p. 50) that _remorata_ "appears to have been more widespread in the past. It is conceivable that hybridization between _remorata_ and _attenuata_ may have led to the origin of the complex known as _muricata_." The evidence that I have gathered indicates that _muricata_ is indeed a hybrid, but a product of _remorata_ and "_borealis_."[4/] The evidence for this conclusion rests on the fossil record which must now be reviewed.

PINUS MASONII DORF

(Plate 12)

Pinus masonii Dorf, Carnegie Inst. Wash. Pub. 412, p. 70, pl. 5, figs.
    4-6 (Pico and Merced Formations), 1930.

Pinus masonii Dorf. Axelrod, Proc. Sympos. Biol. Calif. Islands, p. 117,
    pl. 5, figs. 1, 2, and 4 (Pico Formation); pl. 5, fig. 5 (Lower
    Merced Formation); pl. 6, fig. 2 (Upper Merced Formation), 1967.

Fossil cones of P. masonii Dorf, which have been considered similar

to those of the living P. muricata D. Don (Dorf, 1930; Mason, 1932;

Axelrod, 1967a) occur at several localities in rocks of Miocene and

Pliocene age. In addition, the cones of a species similar to P. masonii

that occur in rocks of Pleistocene age have been identified as the living

P. muricata (Mason, 1932; Chaney and Mason, 1933; Axelrod, 1967a). The

presumed close affinity of all these fossils to the living muricata now

appears to be incorrect. Prior to discussing its relationships, new data

regarding the occurrences of P. masonii at the older sites, and the

allied P. "borealis" in Quaternary rocks, are presented first.

Fossil Records

Pico

(Plate 12, figs. 1 and 2)

The Pico Formation, which is exposed in the Ventura basin of coastal

southern California, has yielded cones at 3 localities. All of them

occur in the lower part of the formation. The sites are at Pitas Pt. and

Punta Gorda on the coast west of Ventura and in the bed of Santa Paula

Creek 3 miles north of that town (Dorf, 1930; Axelrod, 1967a). The age

of the Pico Formation was based earlier on the climatic indications of

marine invertebrates in the section (Dorf, 1930; Durham, 1954; Jennings

and Troxel, 1954), with the replacement of warm- by cold-water taxa

presumably indicating the commencement of the Pleistocene. As reviewed

by Yeats and McLaughlin (1970), the sequence of pelagic foraminifera in

southern California shows that there was an alternation of warm- and

cold-water faunas commencing as far back as 11.5 m.y., or in the Miocene

(Ingle, 1967). The fossil cone localities are stratigraphically well

below a marker ashbed that occurs widely in the thick marine Pico Formation and has been dated at 8.7 ± 0.5 m.y. (Yeats and McLaughlin, 1970). The cones cannot be younger, and an age of about 9 m.y. seems likely (Table 1).

Cones of this alliance appear to be in the Rancho La Brea deposit. Two nearly complete cones were recovered from Pit 91 by Janet Warter, who reports (personal communication, August, 1979) that an associated sample gives a radiocarbon age of 32,000 B.P. The 3 cones known previously from Pit 9 are at depths of 12.5 and 17 ft. (Frost, 1927, p. 76) and are therefore older than 40,000 B.P. (see Berger and Libby, 1966, pp. 492-493). Only one of these is complete (Mason, 1927, pl. 3, fig. 1), the other two being split longitudinally, with the side having the thick scales and prominent apophyses missing. The cones from Rancho La Brea are more robust, more ovate, and fully half again larger than those of P. "borealis" from the Carpinteria and Pt. Sal localities (see below; also Axelrod, 1967a, pl. 7). The Rancho La Brea cones are more nearly like the fragmentary specimens of P. masonii Dorf from the lower Pico Formation (Dorf, 1930, pl. 5, figs. 5 and 6; also see Plate 12, figs. 1 and 2 in this report), and the cone from the Lower Merced Formation (Axelrod, 1967a, pl. 5, fig. 5). Closer comparisons cannot now be made because the record at these localities is so limited. Until more fossil cones become available, it seems best to recognize tentatively that the La Brea pine may be an extinct taxon of the masonii-"borealis" line of evolution, and closer to masonii than to "borealis."

Collection: U.C. Mus. Pal., Paleobot. ser., Cotypes nos. 306, 307.

Merced

(Plate 12, figs. 3 and 4)

The cones from the type section of the Merced Formation, exposed on the outer coast between Mussel Rock and Ft. Funston (San Francisco South Quadrangle, U. S. Geol. Surv. scale 1:24,000, 1947), occur at different localities in the lower part of the formation north of the San Andreas fault. As shown by Glen (1959, p. 163), this part of the Merced is Upper Pliocene, and equivalent in age to the San Joaquin Formation of the Coalinga region as judged from the megafossils available for comparison. The illustrated cones are similar to those from the Pico, and also resemble those from the Late Pleistocene at Carpinteria (Plates 13 and 14) and Pt. Sal (Plates 15 and 16), but are larger.

Collection. U. C. Mus. Pal., Paleobot. ser., Hypotype nos. 159, 20532.

PINUS "BOREALIS" DUFFIELD

(Plates 13-17)

Pinus muricata var. "borealis" Duffield, Interrelationships of the California closed-cone pines, with special reference to Pinus muricata D. Don (Univ. California, Berkeley, Ph.D. thesis; 77 pp.), 1951.

Pinus muricata D. Don. Mason, Madroño 2(6): 51, pl. 1, fig. 3 (Carpinteria), 1932.

Pinus muricata D. Don. Chaney and Mason, Carnegie Inst. Wash. Pub. 415; p. 54, pl. 4, fig. 1 (previously figured by Mason, 1932); pl. 5, fig. 3 (Carpinteria), 1933.

Pinus muricata D. Don. Mason, Carnegie Inst. Wash. Pub. 415: 147, pl. 6, fig. 2; pl. 7, fig. 4 (Millerton), 1934.

Pinus muricata D. Don. Axelrod, Proc. Sympos. Biol. Calif. Islands, p.

　　120, pl. 5, fig. 3 (San Pedro Formation); pl. 6, figs. 3 and 4, and

　　pl. 7, figs. 1-9 (Orcutt Formation), 1967a.

Fossil Records

Carpinteria

(Plates 13 and 14)

Numerous cones at Carpinteria were identified earlier as P. muricata

D. Don by Chaney and Mason (1933). Although they resemble the cones of

P. muricata in some respects, they do not show the range of variation of

that species. This is evident from a comparison of the Carpinteria cones

with a typical suite of muricata cones, as illustrated on Plate 11.

Clearly, the Carpinteria fossils show only one extreme of the variation

of the living muricata.

　　Collections: U.C. Mus. Pal., Paleobot. ser. Hypotype nos. 5924-5929,

homeotype nos. 5930-5947.   Santa Barbara Museum of Natural History,

Hypotype nos. 2,3, 467-472.

Pt. Sal

(Plates 15 and 16)

　　A large number of perfectly preserved cones (some with winged seeds

still intact) have been recovered from the Orcutt Formation near Pt. Sal.

The variation of this suite does not include all of that displayed by the

living muricata (see Plates 11 and 20); there is no evidence, among the

100-odd complete cones, of variation toward the smooth cone scales such

as occur regularly in muricata var. "typica" populations.

　　Collections: U.C. Mus. Pal., Paleobot. ser. Hypotype nos. 5844-5855,

20398-20408, homeotype nos. 5856-5923, 20409-20416.

Millerton

Mason (1934) collected 7 cones from the Millerton Formation that he identified as Pinus muricata. These were recovered from 5 localities (Mason, 1934, p. 89), distributed north-south along Tomales Bay for a distance of 19 km (12 mi). Clearly, this pine was not a common member of the forest in the structural trough where Pinus radiata dominated.

Mason (1934, pl. 6, fig. 2) figured only one ovulate cone and one other is in the collection at the Museum of Paleontology, University of California, Berkeley. There is certainly no evidence from the limited material now available to show that this pine may not represent P. "borealis" rather than P. muricata var. "typica" Duffield.

    Collection: U.C. Mus. Pal., Hypotype nos. 454 (cone), 455 (fascicle).

Discussion

As noted above, P. masonii Dorf was described initially from cones collected from the lower part of the marine Pico Formation near Ventura, and from the lower part of the type Merced Formation in the sea-cliffs north of Mussel Rock, south of San Francisco (Plate 12). All of the fossil cones, whether the few known from the Pico (9 m.y.) and Merced (3-4 m.y.) formations, or the large suites from the Pleistocene deposits referred here to P. "borealis," are alike in that they are strongly asymmetrical and the cone scales are prominently hooked on all specimens (Plates 13-16). The fossil cones (Plates 13 to 16) show only a part of the variation of the living muricata var. "typica" (Plates 11 and 20). The suites of fossil cones do not grade from those that are strongly asymmetrical with hooked apophyses, to those that are moderately or slightly asymmetrical with prominent apophyses, to cones that are fully symmetrical and have plane, thin scales as in remorata. The cones of P.

masonii from the Pliocene and older rocks are few in number (Plate
12), yet all of them are similar to the Late Pleistocene fossils P.
"borealis".   If they were related to muricata var. "typica," then the
probability is high that at least a few of them would show intermediate
relations in terms of variation toward those with smooth symmetrical
cones.   Since the large suites of fossils from Pt. Sal (over 100 complete
cones) and Carpinteria (over 60 cones) do not display the range of
variation of muricata var. "typica," they cannot represent that taxon.

This conclusion is reinforced by the fact that these floras lived on
floodplains.   Since the rivers carried some cones to the sites of accumulation from trees upstream, the fossil suites at these localities were
assembled from numerous trees.   Inasmuch as the collections provide no
evidence of the range of cone variation like that in the living muricata
var. "typica" (see Plate 11), the fossil populations represent a different taxon.   They are here identified as P. "borealis" Duffield because
they resemble it more than any other (see Plate 17).   The distinctness of
P. "borealis" seems even more significant when we note that occasional
rare cones of P. remorata occur both at Carpinteria and Pt. Sal (see
above), yet there is no evidence of intergradation between the species in
those deposits.

Taken at its face value, the evidence indicates that P. masonii
from Pliocene and older rocks, and the similar fossils of "borealis" that
occur more abundantly in upper Pleistocene rocks and have been named
muricata, represent different taxons.   For this reason, all the cones
from the Pleistocene previously identified as muricata are transferred to
P. "borealis" Duffield, as listed above.

PINUS REMORATA MASON

(Plates 18 and 19)

Pinus remorata Mason, Madroño 2: 8-10, 1930

Pinus remorata Mason. Chaney and Mason, Carnegie Inst. Wash. Pub. 415:

10, pl. 6, figs. 1, 2, 1930.

Pinus remorata Mason. Chaney and Mason, Carnegie Inst. Wash. Pub. 415:

56, 1933.

Pinus remorata Mason. Axelrod, Proc. Sympos. Biol. Calif. Islands,

p. 128, pl. 3, fig. 2; pl. 4, figs. 2-4; pl. 5, fig. 6; pl. 8, fig.

3, 1967a.

As noted earlier, the living P. remorata Mason is characterized by
cones that are ovate and symmetrical, the scales are smooth and without
apophyses, and the cones stand normal to the branch. Where it occurs
near muricata, notably on the coastal plain 3 miles south of Cerro
Colorado, which is on the coast west of San Vicente, Baja California,
remorata trees are conspicuously a lighter green, not so dense, and the
branches are normal to the trunk, not as curved upward in their outer
part as in muricata. In addition, remorata branchlets are brittle, not
pliable as in muricata, and the bark is not so deeply furrowed.

Fossil Records

As presently known, the fossil record includes cones from 4 previous
localities and 1 new site. The old sites are: (1) the Willow Creek flora
on Santa Cruz Island (Chaney and Mason, 1930); (2) the Carpinteria flora
(Chaney and Mason, 1933); (3) in a Plio-Pleistocene deposit below street
level at the mouth of Potrero Canyon, Santa Monica (Axelrod, 1967a); and
(4) in the Orcutt Sandstone near Pt. Sal (Axelrod, 1967a). Inasmuch as

as the fossils are not common at these localities, it is desirable to record the occurrence of additional cones at 3 of these sites. The new locality is at Century City in West Los Angeles, as noted below.

Santa Cruz Island

(Plate 19, fig. 2)

Although 9 cones were collected at this site by Chaney and Mason (1930), only two were retained in the type collection. I visited the area in April 1975, and found that the vertical stream-bank from which the principal fossils were recovered has slumped. Although the slide now covers most of the plant-bearing layers, a perfect cone was recovered from the deposit (Plate 19, fig. 2). It is smaller than those figured by Chaney and Mason, but well within the range of variation of the living species.

Collection: U.C. Pal., Paleobot. ser. Hypotype no. 5839.

Carpinteria

(Plate 19, fig. 5)

Two cones of P. remorata were identified by Chaney and Mason in the Carpinteria collection at the Santa Barbara Museum of Natural History. Owing to their rarity as compared with the abundance of cones they identified as P. muricata (= "borealis"; see Discussion above), it was assumed that they were washed ashore, carried as sea drift from Santa Cruz Island. However, the geologist Putnam (1942) has shown that the deposit accumulated in a stream valley, not on a beach.

Examination of additional Carpinteria material at the Santa Barbara Museum of Natural History shows that two additional cones of P. remorata

are in the collection there, the best one of which is illustrated here
(Plate 19, fig. 5).

Collection: Santa Barbara Museum of Natural History. Hypotype no.
474, homeotype no. 7.

Pt. Sal

(Plate 19, fig. 3)

The initial collection at this locality yielded a fragmentary cone
that was referred tentatively to P. remorata (Axelrod, 1967a). On a
recent trip (August 1977) to the site, a perfect cone of remorata was
recovered and was added to the collection.

Collection: U.C. Pal., Paleobot. ser. Hypotype nos. 5840, 20422.

Century City

(Plate 19, figs, 1 and 4)

The excavation for Century City, West Los Angeles, revealed an excel-
lent 10-meter section of siltstone and mudstone. Near the middle there
was a sandstone filled with mollusks of Early Pleistocene or Late Pliocene age, according to Louella R. Saul who has kindly examined the collection at UCLA. Several unaltered cones were recovered by David Weide
and Alan Barrows from the middle part of the excavation and were turned
over to me for study (Plate 19, figs. 1 and 4). One is preserved in the
lime-cemented sandstone filled with mollusks and 3 others were recovered
from the associated shale, all at a depth of 5 m below street level. The
cones are similar to those recovered from an excavation for a gasoline
storage tank on Coast Highway 1 at the mouth of Potrero Canyon, Santa
Monica (Axelrod, 1967a, p. 130). The marine faunas at each site appear
to be contemporaneous, and suggest that P. remorata covered much of the
shore area at that time.

Collection. U.C. Pal., Paleobot. ser. Hypotype nos. 5841 and 5842,

homeotype no 5843.

Discussion

Emphasis is placed again on the fact that at two of these sites

(Carpinteria and Pt. Sal) P. remorata and P. "borealis" (muricata of

authors) occur in the same beds. However, in the large samples (100+

cones) that are now available, there is no evidence of intermediate forms

that might link these taxa. This is possibly due to their genetic isola-

tion, which resulted chiefly from different times of flowering of the

cones. This agrees with the observations of W. B. Critchfield (personal

communication, November 1977), who notes that in cultivation remorata

cones flower earlier (pollen shedding, ovule receptivity) than those of

muricata. This is expectable, because remorata regularly inhabits drier

sites than muricata, as noted above.

PINUS MURICATA D. DON: A RECENT HYBRID

The evidence reviewed above suggests that the muricata-remorata prob-

lem is the result of hybridization between two species, "borealis" (now

relict) and remorata (now relict), and that the hybrid (muricata var.

"typica", is better adapted to present conditions. The evidence that

supports this interpretation can now be summarized. In the first place,

all known fossil cones of P. masonii are markedly asymmetric and have

prominently hooked cone scales on the outer side (Plate 12). This

applies to cones from the Lower Pico Formation (age 9 m.y.), from the

Merced Pliocene (4-5 to 2 m.y.), and especially to those of allied

"borealis" from the rich Late Pleistocene Carpinteria and Pt. Sal locali-

ties (Plates 13-16). As emphasized earlier, there is no evidence of variation toward symmetrically ovate cones with smooth scales as in muricata "typica" populations.

Secondly, all known fossils of remorata have symmetrical cones with smooth, thin scales (Plate 19). None show any transition toward "borealis," even though they occur in the same deposit, as at Carpinteria (Plates 13 and 14) and Pt. Sal (Plates 15 and 16). Cones of the species from the Plio-Pleistocene boundary, dated near 2 m.y., are also typical of the living remorata as shown by the records from Potrero Canyon and Century City. These appear to be contemporaneous, and suggest that the taxon was widely spread along the coastal strip at that time.

The third point is that at present there are no fossil suites of cones that display the range of variation produced by muricata today: the living muricata var. "typica" has no known fossil record.

The presence of two distinctly different species (remorata and "borealis") in the Late Pleistocene, and the occurrence today of the variable muricata var. "typica" populations close to areas where the former two lived as recently as 28,000 years ago, implies that muricata var. "typica" is more recent in origin. Recall that living remorata populations are very rare, being confined to drier sites on Burton Mesa, Santa Rosa and Santa Cruz islands, and in lower Cañon de los Piñitos on the coastal terrace 5 km south of Cerro Colorado (west of San Vicente, Baja California). Muricata var. "typica" also occurs in these areas, but usually in more mesic situations, either at higher elevations (upper Cañon de los Piñitos) or on suitable substrates (e.g., diatomite in Pine Canyon); it is chiefly in intermediate sites that the two taxa are often associated. Note also that although "borealis" occurs in Upper Pleistocene rocks as a dominant species (Pt. Sal, Carpinteria), it still exists,

extending from near Ft. Ross northward (Fig. 6). All the populations
from Marin County southward are typical of muricata var. "typica" because
they show variation toward remorata-type cones. Clearly, muricata var.
"typica" is simply a hybrid of remorata and "borealis"; the extremes
of cone variation in typical muricata var. "typica" populations represent
the normal cones of remorata and "borealis" (Plate 20; also see figures
in Linhart, Burr, and Conkle, 1967).

    Hybridization between "borealis" and remorata may have resulted from
disturbance of the habitat (see Anderson and Stebbins, 1954). In this
case, it probably was initially a response to Late Wisconsin and subsequent climates, and then to the activities of man (clearing, grazing,
fires, etc.). As noted above, remorata regularly inhabits drier sites
where it is adjacent to mixed populations that are the presumed hybrids
(muricata var. "typica"). A trend to warmer and drier climate, and to
more extreme summer temperatures, would favor the spread of remorata into
"borealis" groves, and result in their hybridization. The apparent
absence of any significant record of hybridization at earlier times seems
explicable on an ecologic basis. At Carpinteria, which was dominated by
"borealis" and P. radiata, the rare remorata probably was living on more
remote, drier sites. These were provided by the south-facing massive
sandstone outcrops of the Eocene Sespe, Coldwater, and Matilija formations at the base of the range directly north, and by the well-drained
alluvial fans to which they contributed. It is recalled that the Carpinteria flora also has rare remains of Juniperus, Arctostaphylos, and Pinus
sabiniana that required drier, warmer sites than those on the foggy
coastal strip where Pinus radiata and P. "borealis" dominated the forest.
At Pt. Sal, drier areas were provided by the coarse sandstones and

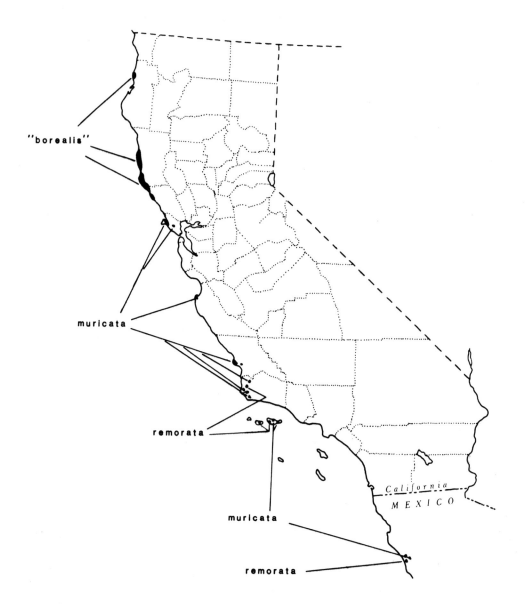

Fig. 6.   Present distribution of taxa of the "muricata complex," as interpreted in this report (map from Griffin and Critchfield, 1972).

conglomerates of the Oligocene Lospe Formation, and by outcrops of
Cretaceous Franciscan Formation nearby to the south, both well removed
from the mesic floodplain that was shrouded in fog. In these drier,
sunnier, warmer areas, cones would have flowered earlier than in the
foggy sites. This could isolate the taxa reproductively, except perhaps
in a narrow ecotone, and distance would militate against remorata's
contributing many cones to the record.

As noted above, the influence of remorata in muricata var. "typica"
populations extends north in diminished amount to Inverness Ridge, Marin
County, but not farther north except for a rare tree in the area from Ft.
Ross northward for a short distance. These may represent relictual
occurrences from the Xerothermic. With the return to a moister, foggier
climate, "borealis" would be better adapted and hence is outcompeting and
swamping out the rare trees of "var. typica." This is consistent with
the robust large trees in the area which Critchfield (1972) has noted
comprise two races that differ in color (blue-green vs. green) and also
differ chemically, but hybridize along a narrow ecotone.

One problem pertains to the source of muricata var. "typica." Is it
the result of the northward penetration of remorata into populations of
"borealis," or did muricata var. "typica" originate in southern or south-
central coastal California? In the latter case, it would have migrated
northward during the waning of the Wisconsin pluvial perod. This explanation seems more plausible, because pure "borealis" populations are at
Pt. Sal and Carpinteria, and were already established there in earlier
times, as well as along the central California coast, as shown by the
records in the Merced Formation near San Francisco. The spread of drier
climate following the Wisconsin would have favored the northward movement

of var. "typica" into areas occupied by "borealis," because it prefers
drier areas.

As the acme of the Xerothermic was reached, the range of all the
coastal pine populations was disrupted (Axelrod, 1966a, p. 53). They
now survive in discontinuous patches along the coast (Fig. 6), chiefly
in areas where strong upwelling produces a heavier fog deck that is more
persistent and frequent than in most of the intervening areas. With the
return to moister, cooler climate following the Xerothermic, muricata
"typica" would tend to genetically swamp out the remaining relict
remorata groves over areas of their occurrence, much as can be seen today
in the hills near Lompoc, on Santa Cruz Island, and near San Vicente.
Relict, pure remorata populations probably were destroyed also by fires,
generated chiefly by man's activities during the past 300 years, notably
in Baja California and coastal southern California. The trees are relatively small as compared with the larger, more luxuriant muricata var.
"typica," and they regularly have a dense understory of sclerophyllous
shrubs that burn readily and would destroy the small trees and their
thin-scaled cones.

HISTORY OF PINUS Subsect. OOCARPEAE

Age

The fossil records of members of the Oocarpeae in California and
Nevada have been reviewed earlier (Axelrod, 1967a). Two important new
items have now been added to that discussion. As presented above, one
concerns the revised age for the Pico Formation, and its bearing on the 9
m.y. age of P. masonii Dorf cones from localities in the Ventura basin.
The second item is the discovery of a rich deposit of fossil Monterey
pine cones (Pinus lawsoniana Axelrod) in the Drakes Bay Formation, dated

3.5 m.y. Apart from these occurrences (see Table 1), the oldest records
are provided by pollen from the Wilmington Core in the Los Angeles area
(Martin and Gray, 1962, fig. 2), the basal part of which reaches down
into Temblor-Barstovian time (14-15 m y.).   The pollen of the pine is
abundant and is definitely that of the closed-cone pine group, according
to Dr. W. S. Ting (verbal report of 1963).   Most of the pollen in the
lower part of the section is similar to "muricata" (= masonii), though
P. attenuata also appears to be present in small amount.   One other
indication of the antiquity of the group is provided by two silicified
cones of a Monterey pine, generally small in size, that probably were
collected from the Monterey Formation in Santa Barbara, as noted earlier.
Not shown in Table 1 or Figure 4 are numerous Late Pleistocene records
from the coastal strip (see Axelrod, 1967 a and b).   It is amply clear
that the history of the subsect. Oocarpeae extends well down into the
Tertiary.

Source

     The area of early differentiation of the group can be inferred from
two lines of evidence, tectonic and floristic.   The former is based on
the precepts of plate tectonics, the latter on the past and present links
of woody taxa associated with closed-cone pine forests in California and
Mexico.

Tectonic evidence

     Cumulative separation on the San Andreas fault system in central
California has totaled 450-500 km since the Early Miocene (Figs. 7-9).
This is evident from the offset of identical volcanic-sedimentary
sequences of the Pinnacles and Neenach Formations which lie on opposite

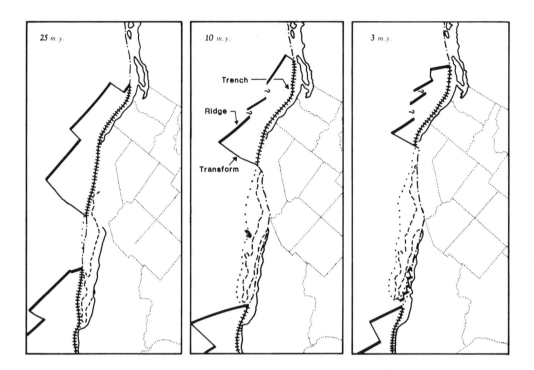

Fig. 7.   Opening of the Gulf of California during the middle and late Neogene (simplified from Smith, 1976).   Comparison with Figs. 8 and 9 suggests that the California maritime taxa have been displaced north-ward, away from their relatives in Mexico (also see Beck and Plumley, 1979).

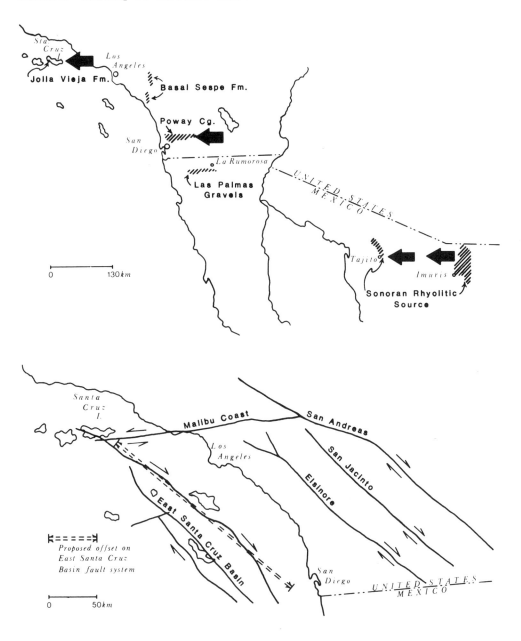

Fig. 8. Showing (above) the rhyolitic conglomerates displaced northwesterly from their Sonoran source area, and (below) the major fault systems in southern California and the inferred offset in the insular region (simplified from Abbott and Smith, 1978).

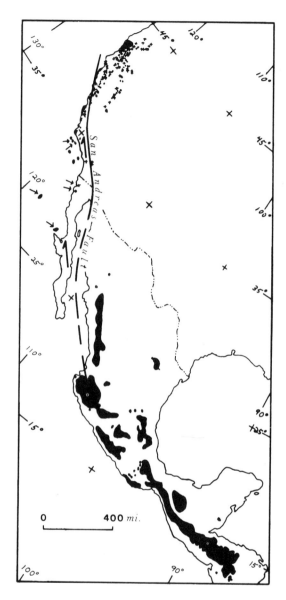

Fig. 9.   Distribution of 8 species of <u>Pinus</u> subsect. Oocarpeae (from Little and Critchfield, 1969, Map 22). Note that the Californian species are separated from the Mexican taxa by the Gulf of California and the Sonoran Desert, as well as by latitude. Furthermore, with Baja California in its Miocene position (see Figure 7), Guadalupe and Cedros islands (marked by arrows) are placed close to the mainland and to the other species of Oocarpeae.

sides of the rift (Smith, 1977; Matthews, 1976; also Kovach and Nur,

1973).   A comparable displacement is indicated for the San Andreas in

southern California, as the Mint Canyon basin has been displaced north-

westerly from the Orocopia-Chocolate Mountains area since 12-13 m.y.

(Crowell, 1962, 1975; Ehlert and Ehlig, 1977; Ehlig, Ehlert, and Crowe,

1975; also Smith, 1977).

In southern California and adjacent Baja California, the insular and

maritime pines are separated from the San Andreas by several faults,

notably the Elsinore, San Jacinto, San Clemente, Hosgri, and Agua Dulce,

on which there has also been lateral movement.   Cumulative slip is not

yet established, but tentative estimates (e.g. Seiders, 1978; Graham and

Dickinson, 1978) indicate a series of shuffling blocks (Johnson and

Normark, 1974) moving northwesterly may have a total offset of about 200

km.   This estimate is supported further by a recent study of rhyolite

tuff clasts which are abundant in the Eocene conglomerates of the coastal

plain of Baja California and southern California, and on 4 of the Channel

Islands (Abbott and Smith, 1978).   Statistical comparison of the trace

element composition of rhyolite suites from 5 areas indicates that the

rhyolitic bedrock and conglomerate clasts in north-central Sonora were a

part of the source terrane for the nonmarine and shallow marine Eocene

Poway Conglomerate of the San Diego area, and also of the deep water

marine Eocene conglomerate on Santa Cruz Island.   The data strongly

suggest that the Sonoran, Poway, and Santa Cruz Island rhyolites are

genetically related, and that the system has been dismembered tectonic-

ally by opening of the Gulf of California and major strike-slip displace-

ment of the southern California borderland.   This indicates a lateral

movement of about 250 km (160 mi.) on faults in the borderland area (San

Diego to Santa Cruz Island) since the late Eocene, as depicted in Fig. 8.

If we restore the slices west of the San Andreas to their position in the middle Miocene (Gastil, Phillips, and Rodriguez-Torres, 1972; Gastil and Jensky, 1973), and recall that sea-floor spreading in the Sea of Cortez commenced about 6-8 m.y. ago (Karig and Jensky, 1972; D.G. Moore, 1973), then the present populations of Oocarpeae in southern California and adjacent Baja California were aligned along the coast of Sonora-Sinaloa-Jalisco, close to the species of Oocarpeae now there, and linked to the others via the mountains of central and eastern Mexico (compare Fig. 7 with Fig. 9). Tectonic evidence thus suggests the mountains of Mexico as the probable region of early Oocarpeae evolution. This fulfills the evolutionary requirements of an area of continental diversity, as inferred earlier (Axelrod, 1958, 1967a). The postulated diversity of the group in the Miocene thus approximates that exhibited by the 10 species of subsect. Ponderosae in that region today. Tectonic evidence also clarifies the reason for the existence of 2 very distinct groups within subsecy. Oocarpeae, of which the California taxa are chiefly maritime, and the Mexican are mostly montane and interior, as is one of the California species (attenuata). It also implies that the California maritime group was largely transported northward by complex movements on the San Andreas fault system, commencing in the Late Miocene.

Floristic evidence

The Miocene and Pliocene floras of California and border areas contain taxa related to species that are now in the mountains of southern Baja California, in the Sierra Madre Occidental, or in both areas (see review in Axelrod, 1958; 1967b). Among the species in the Miocene of southern California (marked *) that have relict occurrences in southern

Baja California are *Arbutus peninsularis and *Quercus brandegeei.

Woodland taxa in the Cape Region that are also in western Mexico include

Ilex discolor var. tolucana, Quercus albocincta, Q. reticulata, Q.

tuberculata, *Populus brandegeei and Rhus tepetate. California taxa in

the Cape Region are represented by *Heteromeles arbutifolia, *Malosma

laurina, *Platanus racemosa, and *Populus fremontii, all in the Neogene

of California. There are also groups of related species (phylads)

ranging from California southward into the Cape Region, across the

southwestern United States, and into northern Mexico, that provide

evidence for the former continuity of diverse ancestral groups over the

region. Included here are:

> Cupressus nevadensis-arizonica-forbesii-guadalupensis
>
> Juniperus californica-monosperma-erythrocarpa
>
> Pinus monophylla-edulis-cembroides-quadrifolia
>
> Garrya fremontii-ovata-laurifolia
>
> Platanus racemosa-wrightii
>
> Populus fremontii (and its varieties)-mexicana
>
> Quercus wislizenii-emoryi-peninsularis-devia

Furthermore, a number of genera that are now only in western Mexico or in

the southwestern United States (or in both areas) that have records in

the Miocene and Pliocene of California. Among these are Clethra,

Dodonaea, Ilex, Magnolia, Persea, Robinia, Sabal, Sapindus, and others

that disappeared during the Pliocene as summer rains were reduced. Last-

ly, it is recalled that some taxa that occur with the present California

closed-cone pines have close allies in the mountains of western Mexico,

where they occur with other members of the Oocarpeae. Among these

paired-species are Arbutus menziesii-xalapensis, Ceanothus arboreuscoeruleus, Cercocarpus traskiae-mojadensis, Comarostaphylis diversifolia-many spp., Garrya fremontii-ovata, and Vaccinium ovatum-confertum. Some of them which have equivalents in the fossil record were already similar to living species by the Miocene, and probably earlier. Manifestly, the taxa of the woody flora have for the most part been relatively stable since the Miocene, including some species of Arctostaphylos (e.g., glauca, glandulosa, pungens) and Ceanothus (e.g., cuneatus, crassifolius, verrucosus). It was the taxa of the annual and perennial herbaceous flora that evolved at a particularly rapid rate in the later Pliocene and especially in the Quaternary (Stebbins and Major, 1965; Axelrod, 1966a; Raven and Axelrod, 1977). This was in response to an increasingly more dynamic physical environment brought on by the coincidence of major tectonism and notable climatic fluctuations that resulted in rapidly shifting populations, much hybridization, and further radiation into the expanding new habitats.

The closed-cone pines of coastal California have survived in a maritime situation where water-stress in summer is reduced by the fog that shelters the groves from the hot summer sun. It provides not only a low range of very mild temperature, but the drip from the trees keeps the ground moist and cool. These conditions appear to compensate for the lack of adequate summer rainfall which characterized the present area of California pines into the Early Pleistocene. Their survival here is not due to their fortuitous occurrence in an environment that is widely different from that in which the related Mexican members of the Oocarpeae have survived. The taxa in each region live under equable temperatures, with Pinus oocarpa ranging into the warmest climates. All the mainland Mexican species inhabit an area that has ample summer rain, a feature that gradually disappeared from California during the Pliocene together with the floristic links that were formerly here.

A Tentative Phyletic Scheme

The fossil record as now known illuminates only dimly the early evolutionary relations of the species of the group.   The evidence that indicates a slow rate of evolution in the Oocarpeae during the Tertiary is paralleled by that indicated for species of other subsections of Pinus in the western United States.   Table 4, updated from an earlier listing (Axelrod, 1967a), presents the oldest records now known of fossil pines similar to several living species in the United States. Clearly, stability has been a major feature of pine evolution, not only in the western United States, but also in western and southern Europe and eastward (see Gaussen, 1960; Mirov, 1967).   This stability has been in spite of major environmental changes which have restricted taxa and forced many to adapt to wholly new climates of greater cold, or drought, or to a different growing season in Mediterranean climate regions.   Such changes must have been accompanied by physiologic modifications that have enabled the taxa to persist.   It is therefore amply clear that in order to interpret phylogeny of the Oocarpeae, fossils from rocks of Middle Miocene and greater age are needed.   In spite of the lack of record, a few tentative suggestions can be made if we keep in mind the tectonic and climatic changes of the middle and later Tertiary.

The Oocarpeae comprise two subgroups, Mexican and Californian (Fig. 10).   Both can evidently be related to an ancestral form analogous to Pinus oocarpa, for it includes variation that can be considered proto-typic of both subgroups (see illustrations in Martinez, 1948; Shaw, 1914).   One evolutionary line with long-elliptic cones was chiefly

Table 4.   Ages of fossil pines allied to modern taxa in the western United States.
(These pines lend support to the inference that the California maritime pines of
the Oocarpeae also have considerable antiquity)

Fossil Species	Similar Living Species	Occurrence and Reference	Age (m. y.)
Subsect. FLEXILES			
Pinus florissanti Lesq.	P. flexilis	Florissant, Colo. (MacGinitie, 1953)	35
Subsect. BALFOURIANEAE			
P. balfouroides Axelrod	P. balfouriana	Thunder Mt., Ida. (UCMP)	27
		Purple Mt., Nev. (UCMP)	13
		Chalk Hills, Nev. (UCMP)	12
P. crossii Knowlton	P. aristata	Copper Basin, Nev. (Axelrod, 1966b)	40
		Creede, Colo. (Knowlton, 1923)	27
Subsect. PONDEROSAE			
P. sturgisi Cockerell	P. ponderosa	Green River, Colo. (MacGinitie, 1969)	47
		Florissant, Colo. (MacGinitie, 1953)	35
		Bakersfield, Calif.; (UCMP)	14
		Fingerrock, Nev. (Wolfe, 1964)	16
		Fallon, Nev. (Axelrod, 1956)	12
Subsect. STROBUS			
P. prelambertiana Axelrod	P. lambertiana	Del Mar, Calif. (UCMP)	50
Subsect. CEMBROIDES			
P. ballii Brown	P. cembroides (group)	Green River, Colo. (MacGinitie, 1969)	45
Subsect. CONTORTEAE			
*P. elkoana Axelrod	P. contorta (group)	Bull Run, Nev. (UCMP)	40

UCMP = Univ. California Museum of Paleontology, Berkeley

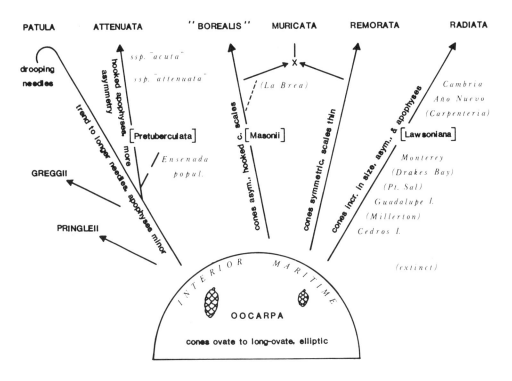

Fig. 10   Interrelationships of taxa of the Oocarpeae may be considered in terms of two subgroups diverging from a variable, <u>Pinus oocarpa</u>-like plexus, probably in Oligocene time (Tertiary species in brackets).

continental and gave rise to the closely related species greggii-patula-pringleii in the mountains of Mexico. In this group there is a trend to longer needles; but the cones, which are long-elliptic, do not develop prominent swollen or hooked apophyses. However, an offshoot that reached California as P. pretuberculata Axelrod (cf. attenuata) by the late Miocene (11 m.y.) became progressively more armed with larger, hooked apophyses. The southernmost attenuata stand, which is east of Ensenada, provides a morphologic link between the attenuata populations of California and the Mexican greggii (Newcomb, 1962), which chemical evidence indicates are closely related (Mirov, 1967). The less pronounced development of apophyses on cones in the Ensenada population (Newcomb, 1962, fig. 11) may reflect the more frequent occurrence of summer rain in that area, as compared with southern California with its longer, drier summers. This agrees with the decrease in apophyses development in the northern California variant that Newcomb (1962) designated spp. attenuata and which also inhabits a moister region. This interpretation is further supported by the poor development of apophyses in the other members of the group in Mexico, where summer rains are characteristic.

The second group with ovoid cones, which evidently lived under a more equable maritime climate, shows two trends. In the radiata plexus, the trend in California has been to 3-needled fascicles and to larger cones with greater asymmetry and with increasingly more swollen umbos that terminate in the Cambria variant--all possibly a response to the emergence of a dry summer climate. By contrast, the Guadalupe and Cedros island pines, which regularly receive summer rainfall, are chiefly 2-needled, have the smallest cones in the plexus, and apophyses are not prominently developed. The second trend is represented by the comparatively stable masonii-"borealis" and remorata lines, which recently produced the

aggressive hybrid muricata var. "typica" that has largely displaced both

parents.   The northern "borealis" probably is an ancient taxon. Apart

from additional fossil records, these suggested interrelations may be

tested, at least in part, by chemosystematic studies (e.g. Zavarin,

Snajberk, and Fisher, 1975; Wilson, Carlson, and White, 1977).

COEVOLUTION AND CONE MORPHOLOGY: NEED FOR

AN HISTORICAL APPROACH

It has been suggested that the trend to larger cones with more

swollen apophyses represents an adaptation to aridity and to the frequent

occurrence of fire (Shaw, 1914; Linhart, Burr, and Conkle, 1967, p. 174).

More recently, Linhart (1978) expanded this thesis and suggested that

predation by squirrels may also have resulted in the development of

thicker-scaled cones (in radiata), or in the heavier armament and greater

asymmetry (in muricata, attenuata) in the California Oocarpeae.   A

similar story has been presented by Smith (1970) for coevolution of pine

squirrels and the conifers Douglas fir (Pseudotsuga) and lodgepole pine

(Pinus contorta).   In addition, Smith suggests that the development of

woody conifer cones may have resulted from animal predation earlier in

their history.

In considering these problems, neither Linhart nor Smith has taken

into account the fossil record of Cenozoic conifers or squirrels, or the

geologic and climatic history of the regions they have considered.   These

data provide a different perspective to the general problem of coevolu-

tion of rodents and conifers, and are reviewed here.

Early History

Smith recalls that Florin (1951) showed that the scales of existing conifer cones evolved from dwarf shoots by a process of fusion and reduction in the number of appendages of these shoots. The dwarf shoots contained some ovule-bearing appendages which are homologous with the present ovules and seeds. The bracts that subtended the dwarf shoots are homologous to the bracts of present conifer cones.

The gradual conversion of the leaf-like dwarf shoot appendages into woody cone scales is, according to Smith, unlikely to have occurred in response to the selective pressures exerted by a progressive change in the physical environment that favored a harder and tighter covering for the delicate seed. He believes it is more likely that animals feeding on the seeds became progressively more efficient in finding and extracting the seeds from behind the dwarf shoot or scale, and exerted a progressively stronger selective pressure for hard, tight-fitting scales.

In the late Paleozoic and early Mesozoic Eras, insects, and possibly small mammal-like reptiles, would have been the available predators to initiate the fusion of dwarf-shoot appendages, resulting ultimately in the genus _Pinus_, which probably dates from the late Jurassic (Mirov, 1967; Gaussen, 1960) and was certainly established in the Early Cretaceous (Miller, 1976, 1977). In the Jurassic, multituberculates--a group of rodent-like mammals--enter the fossil record at about the time that conifers with multiappendaged dwarf shoots start to appear. The multituberculates probably were competitively replaced by rodents and other placental herbivores in the late Paleocene and Eocene. Many modern genera and near-modern species in the pine family appear at about this time, including species of _Abies_, _Larix_, _Picea_, _Pinus_, _Pseudolarix_,

Pseudotsuga, and Tsuga.   Smith notes that placental rodents probably were more efficient foragers than multituberculates because of increased thermal regulation and a superior limb positioning for arboreal movement. These advantages would have enabled them to exert a greater selective pressure on cone morphology, with evolution proceeding in the same direction--toward greater protection for the ovules and seeds.   The first rodents in the fossil record, which appear in the late Paleocene, are the squirrel-like Paramyidae, and they disappear in the early Miocene as modern squirrels (Sciuridae) increase in number.   This could also be a case of competitive replacement by a more efficient group.

That some terrestrial animals would have been specializing as seed-eaters from an early date is expectable in view of the high nutritive and caloric value of seeds.   As Smith emphasizes, other animals may also exert selective pressures on conifer reproduction.   He refers to several groups of insects that eat the seeds of most species of conifers in western North America.   Some use only one seed per larva, but others have larva that mine through several seeds per cone.   In some, the insects oviposit between the scales to the area of the seeds, and in others the larvae burrow in.   The length of the scale and speed of its growth are under a finely balanced selective pressure exerted by the length of the ovipositors or the energy available for a larva to mine its way into the seed and out to the surface of the cone.   Selective pressures are also exerted by birds such as crossbills, for whether the upper mandible crosses to the right or left determines the manner in which the bird holds the cone.   Among the different species of crossbills, those with heavier bills utilize species of conifer with hard cones.

These observed and inferred relations raise the question whether diverse animals have guided the evolution of the cone structure, or whether they adapted to cones that were already in existence--and if so, what made the cones? To rely solely on animals feeding on nutrient-rich seeds or ovules overlooks what appears to be an overriding, all-pervasive environmental factor, the climate. The early conifers of the later Paleozoic lived at a time of climatic stress. The continents were then joined into the supercontinent Pangaea, seaways were highly restricted in area, and seasonal drought conditions were widespread. Drought may well have had a significant role in the evolution of the woody cone. It has been pointed out that drought has been a major factor in angiosperm evolution (Stebbins, 1952, 1974). Not only has this inolved dry climate, but there were subcontinental tracts of exposed, ultra-hard Precambrian rocks that were edaphically dry (Axelrod, 1972). These conditions (climatic and edaphic drought) may well have contributed to the transformation of a seed fern-like ancestor into an early angiosperm by closure of the open cupule to protect the ovule and seed (Axelrod, 1970, p. 282). In the same way, thickening of the scales of conifers to provide protection of the exposed ovules from dessication also seems likely. Furthermore, under the selective pressure of climatic and edaphic drought, rate of evolution would be greatly speeded up, as compared with more normal conditions (Axelrod, 1967c). Inasmuch as climate (temperature, rainfall) also largely determines time of flowering, to ignore its role in the evolution of conifer reproductive structures seems gratuitous.

Later History

Recalling that diverse conifer genera were already established by the close of the Eocene, the question arises as to what influence rodents

or other animals may have had on their history since that time.   Two
papers that deal with this problem will be reviewed, because they point
up the difficulties of establishing coevolution of animals and species of
Pinus or other conifers.

Smith (1970) states that the change in the characteristics of lodgepole pines, Douglas firs, and squirrels from the east to the west side of
the Cascade Mountains in southern British Columbia illustrates the factors influencing their evolution.   The Cascades create a rainshadow,
so that the area to the east is dry and fires are frequent.   There,
lodgepole pine (P. contorta) is a common tree, usually occurring in
even-aged stands that have resulted from fire.   The cones on the trees
remain closed for several years after they mature (termed serotinous),
presumably as an adaptation to reseed areas after fire.   The cones serve
as an all-year food supply for squirrels that maintain a relative stable
population.   Douglas fir is the other important tree in this area and
succeeds lodgepole pine in seral succession.   In contrast to lodgepole
pine, Douglas fir may have very large cone crops interspersed with nearly
complete cone-crop failure.   The squirrels switch from their preferred
diet of Douglas fir seeds to lodgepole pine seeds during times of Douglas
fir cone failure.   The drop in squirrel populations is probably dependent
on the relative proportions of Douglas fir and lodgepine pine in mixed
forests.

By contrast, lodgepole pine is rare west of the Cascades, the cones
are not closed, and they may exhibit crop failures.   The squirrel populations fluctuate to a greater degree and they do not exploit as large a
percentage of the cone crops.   Therefore, according to Smith, they exert
a greater selective pressure on cone anatomy east of the Cascades than to

the west. He contends that the effect of their selective pressure east of the range is to make lodgepole pine cones harder in texture and to reduce the number of seeds per cone in Douglas fir. The harder lodgepole pine cones, in turn, exert a selective pressure for squirrels with stronger jaw musculature. As a result, red squirrels (Tamiasciurus hudsonicus) east of the Cascades have a stronger jaw musculature than the Douglas squirrels (T. douglasii) west of the range. Smith (1970, p. 350) concludes that "the causal chain of selective pressures starts with the frequency of fires leading to closed cones, then to increased selective pressures from squirrels for hard cones with fewer seeds, which finally selects for squirrels with strong jaws."

There are a number of reasons why the coevolutionary sequence visualized by Smith probably has not been in operation.

1.   Cones of lodgepole pine similar to those in the interior were already in existence in the Eocene, as shown by an occurrence in the Bull Run flora, northeastern Nevada, in rocks dated at 40 m.y.   It is not certain that the cones were serotinous (=closed), but there is no evidence to show that they were not. The fact that they are very rare in the deposit, though its winged seeds are common, implies that they may have been retained on trees and thus represent an interior form that gave rise to the present subspecies latifolia Critchfield.

Cones of Douglas fir similar to those of the interior var. glauca were already in existence in the late Oligocene, as shown by their occurrence in the Creede flora of Colorado, dated at 27 m.y. This smaller-coned (average length = 2 in.; 5+ cm), fewer-seeded taxon is also in the Purple Mountain flora of western Nevada, dated at 13 m.y.

(Axelrod, 1976b). Both floras lived under a subhumid climate with summer
rainfall. A number of associates of Pseudotsuga in the Purple Mountain
flora, and in floras of similar age in the nearby area, have their
nearest allies in the Rocky Mountains, where var. glauca finds best
development. Furthermore, at the same time, the larger-coned var.
menziesii is recorded in the Miocene Trout Creek flora of Oregon (Arnold,
1935), where it lived under a more humid, equable climate associated with
taxa that are now found chiefly in the coastal strip, including species
of Chamaecyparis, Thuja, Tsuga, Sequoia, Lithocarpus, and others.

Judging from these fossil records, the present populations of
Tamiasciurus east and west of the Cascades could not have had any influence on the development of the present varieties of Pseudotsuga and Pinus
contorta east and west of the Cascades in the Pacific Northwest, as Smith
maintains.

2.   To appraise the impact of tree squirrels on the evolution of
cones of these conifers, certain conclusions reached earlier by special-
ists on these rodents, both living and fossil, must also be considered.
The family Sciuridae reaches well down into Orellan time (30 m.y.), and
Sciurus appears in the Arikareean (22-23 m.y.) as shown by Black (1963,
fig. 7; Evernden and others (1964). Black (p. 240) also notes that "the
early Miocene tree squirrels have changed remarkably little in their
dentition over the past twenty million years." As to the age of the
related Tamiasciurus, its record is more limited, since it is chiefly a
tree-dweller. Black (1963, fig. 7) indicates that it may reach down into
Hemphillian time (7-8 m.y.). In this regard, Moore (1961, p. 11) points
out that the tree squirrel niche of the Boreal forest is occupied by
Tamiasciurus, which is a member of a tribe distinct from Sciurus. Moore

suggests (1959) that its nearest relative may be the little-known rock squirrel of China, _Sciurotamias davidianus_, from which it shows strong generic differences: both represent the tribe Tamiasciurini. If a close relation does exist, then the age of the American _Tamiasciurus_ must be Miocene or older, for forests reached across the Bering region at that time, when an ancestral form of both may have bridged the area. Considering the age of the conifers, and the probable age of the squirrels as well, it seems highly likely that squirrels had adapted to feeding on conifer seeds long before the present Rocky Mountains in British Columbia had been elevated to form a major climatic-biotic boundary in that area.

3. The climatic and vegetation differences east and west of the Cascades in British Columbia only originated after the building up of the range in the late Tertiary and in the early Quaternary. Furthermore, the entire area was under ice as recently as 12,000 years ago. In the Middle Miocene, the area supported a rich mixed deciduous hardwood forest with evergreens and lowland conifers (_Cephalotaxus_, _Taxodium_) that required a climate of high rainfall and equable temperatures. Conifer hardwood forests were then confined to higher, cooler elevations (see Axelrod, 1968, fig. 7). If _Tamiasciurus_ was then in the region, it probably was utilizing other food sources, much as it does today in the eastern United States.

4. _T. hudsonicus_ ranges widely over eastern North America, from the north-central United States (Iowa, Indiana, Illinois, Ohio) northward into the Boreal forest. It inhabits the oak-hickory forest in the eastern United States and the conifer hardwood forest near the Canadian

border.   These forests have walnut, hickory, several oaks, maple (and no doubt others) that Smith (1970, table 6) lists as regular food sources for T. hudsonicus.   These and similar trees were represented in the Cascade region in the Oligocene and Miocene, and were gradually confined coastward and finally eliminated as summer rains decreased in the Plio-cene.   May not T. hudsonicus have developed its more powerful musculature and stronger jaws, as compared with T. douglasii, by feeding on nuts and similar sorts of foods early in its history?   Nuts and acorns would provide a more favorable food source than pitchy conifer cones, as judged from Smith's observations (1970, p. 359):   they do not like pitchy cones. The cones may be a secondary source in the West and in areas farther north, for the occurrence of red squirrel in the Boreal forest must be recent, as the forest itself is largely of post-Tertiary origin.

In this connection, the late Wisconsinian spruce forest that charac-terized much of Minnesota and the Middle West differed from the modern Boreal forest of Canada in the absence of pine, in the apparent mixture of hardwoods (black ash, oak, elm), and in the presence of stands of Artemisia in forest openings (Amundson and Wright, 1979).   Spruce forest was replaced abruptly about 10,000 B.P. by birch, alder, and temperate hardwoods before pine (jack pine?) entered the region for a brief period. Spruce and hardwoods then declined about 9,000 B.P. as pine (red pine?) increased.   Furthermore, charcoal evidence provides no support for the notion that increased fire incidence explains the forest transformation from spruce to pine, according to Amundson and Wright (1979).

5.   The notion that fire has had a role in the development of the differences in taxa east and west of the Cascade Range overlooks the fact that Pinus contorta has spread chiefly since the 1880's under the influ-

ence of uncontrolled forest fires following logging. As a result, lodgepole pine has assumed the role of a weed, supplanting areas of mixed forest that earlier covered the region. The stands of lodgepole pine are now so dense that mixed forests can scarcely become established. Another important factor in the spread of lodgepole has been the overgrazing of meadows, followed by their erosion, the lowering of water table, and the invasion of lodgepole pine into these areas that earlier were too wet for them. Surely, there could not have been sufficient fires in the past 10,000 years (since ice disappeared) to have affected the changes that are now seen east and west of the Cascades.

The Cascades of British Columbia mark a major climatic and biotic boundary (Bailey, 1964, fig. 3; O.E. Baker, 1936; Daubenmire, 1943). The moist, temperate conifer rain-forest to the west lives under relatively mild climate, whereas the more open Pseudotsuga-pine forests to the east inhabit a drier region and one of considerably greater temperature extremes. The fact that lodgepole pine, Douglas fir, and species of Tamiasciurus differ on opposite sides of the range expresses their earlier history, for the present coastal taxa retreated seaward as precipitation decreased and temperature ranges increased over the interior. To assert that the present topographic-climatic boundaries have been involved in the history of these taxa is clearly unwarranted, as the fossil record also demonstrates.

Turning now to the problem of the cone morphology of California Oocarpeae, it has been suggested that the thick-scaled serotinous (= closed) cones that are tightly appressed to the branches may be an adaptation to protect the seeds from fire (Shaw, 1914; Linhart, Burr, and Conkle, 1967, p. 174). More recently, Linhart (1978) has expanded on this thesis and points out that there is also a relation to squirrel predation.   As Linhart notes, cones of the Californian Oocarpeae range from thin-scaled and attached to the branches at relatively right angles (Pinus remorata), to having very thick scales and prominent apophyses (P. attenuata, P. radiata, esp. Ano Nuevo and Cambria populations) on one side and attached to the branches at an acute angle.   Thick-scaled cones provide more protection for the seeds from the high temperatures of forest fires than do thin-scaled cones and may also deter attacks by the squirrels Tamiasciurus and Sciurus.   The thick-scaled cones also have fewer seeds per given weight per cone, which is energetically less effi-cient for the squirrels to harvest; they are known to feed selectively on cones carrying more seeds per cone.   Thin-scaled cones yield more seeds per given cone weight, which is advantageous to reproductive success but may make them a target for squirrels.

Linhart argues that in northern, more mesic areas of California, fires are relatively infrequent, hence there is a fuel buildup, and fires, when they occur, are much hotter than in more southern, xeric areas.   Since in the arid areas fires are more frequent, there is not as much buildup of fuel between fires as there is in more mesic areas, and fires are not as hot.   His point, therefore, is that wherever there are frequent fires, as in dry southern areas, the fires are cooler, and hence seeds can be protected by cones with thinner scales.   Linhart concludes that trees with thin-scaled cones can only be favored in areas where fires are not too hot and where squirrels are rare to absent.   He notes that such conditions occur for the pine populations on Santa Cruz, Santa Rosa, Guadalupe and Cedros islands, and near San Vicente and Ensenada, Baja California.   In these populations, cones with thin scales are most frequent and squirrels are absent.   In areas where fires may be expected to be hotter and squirrels are more common, individuals with thick-scaled, asymmetric cones predominate.

The relations proposed by Linhart can be countered with a number of relationships that weaken his suggested correlation between squirrels, fire, and cone evolution in the California Oocarpeae.

1.   Fires are indeed more frequent in southern California and Baja California, where they have been regularly set for over 300 years.   Some areas are burned every few years.   In spite of this, these fires are indeed hot, for the ground is left barren and the rocks are often burned brick-red by the scorching heat.   Furthermore, the southern pines, due perhaps to lower rainfall as well as to genetic differences, are not so tall as in the north and they are therefore readily torched by flames in the chaparral, which typically include the large shrub Adenostema with its resinous herbage that ignites readily. The fact that both pines-- remorata and muricata--occur in proximity, and are associated with dense chaparral in the Purisima Hills and in the area west of San Vicente, tends to weaken Linhart's argument.   Furthermore, the characters of remorata were established long ago, well before chaparral became a widespread and dominant community (Axelrod, 1975), and before major fires were frequent.

Concerning the frequency and size of fires, an important study by Kilgore and Taylor (1979) seems applicable to the present problem.   As they note, in the mixed conifer forest of the southern Sierra Nevada, most pre-1875 fires were small and of low intensity.   Even the larger ones were confined usually to one slope or one drainage basin.   The mean short intervals between fires suggests that pre-1875 mixed conifer forests did not usually have a thick accumulation of litter or dense brushy thickets under the trees. Instead, small-acreage, low-intensity surface fires consumed accumulated litter at frequent intervals, at the same time killing much of the conifer regeneration which had become established after earlier fires. As they note, frequent small fires would lead to an intricate mosaic of age classes and vegetation subtypes, which in turn would insure that a subsequent fire would not burn large areas with the great intensity of crown fires. In the terrain areas of southern California and Baja California, fires in pre-Spanish times must also have been confined to relatively local areas, on slopes in canyons chiefly. With an absence of dense chaparral like that of today, and with scattered brush species under the stands of trees, thin-scaled conifer cones, like those of remorata and the attenuata stand east of Ensenada, would not be affected seriously.

Since fires have become an important element in upsetting existing ecosystems only in recent times, it is unlikely that they have been a major factor in the evolution of closed-cone pines. However, it does seem likely that intense and frequent large fires during the past few hundred years have destroyed preexisting relict stands of closed-cone pine along the coast, just as fires have eliminated numerous stands of Pseudotsuga macrocarpa from low elevations in the mountains of interior southern California.

2. Fossil Monterey pines with cones as small as those on Guadalupe Island inhabited the mainland during the Pliocene and late Pleistocene (Figs. 2,3; Plates 2 and 7). Hence, the presumed role of squirrels feeding on mainland pines, and stimulating them to develop larger, more asymmetric cones with larger, more protective apophyses, as compared with

the squirrel-free insular populations with smaller, more symmetrical

cones with thin scales, is vitiated, unless one insists that all this

change (Guadalupe to Cambria in size) took place in scarcely 28,000

years. Furthermore, if such a correlation existed, the mainland popula-

tions might be expected to provide evidence of a relationship between

cone- and squirrel-size. The cones of the Cambria population are half

again as large as those of the Monterey population and are much heavier

(Plate 1), yet there are no measurable differences between the squirrel

populations that feed on the cones in these areas (personal communica-

tion from W.Z. Lidicker, of the Museum of Vertebrate Zoology, Univ.

California, Berkeley).

Furthermore, the groves at Monterey, Año Nuevo, and Cambria are well

removed from the recurrent hot fires that regularly sweep through the

chaparral that surrounds Oocarpeae pines in southern California and Baja

California. Noteworthy in this regard is the occurrence of Pinus

attenuata D. Don in the mountains east of Ensenada, where the population

is literally buried in dense chaparral. The cones of this population are

not as prominently deflexed and the cone scales are not as swollen as the

attenuata populations in southern and central California (Newcomb, 1962).

In addition, as noted above, in the coastal strip southwest of Ensenada,

P. remorata is buried in chaparral, and the area is burned repeatedly

by residents. There are no squirrels in the area, but their absence

is comparatively recent, for both Tamiasciurus and Sciurus are in the

San Pedro Martir Range to the south. They no doubt reached that area

together with the montane conifer forest that shifted southward during a

pluvial stage of the Quaternary, a time when the forest boundary was

about 1,000 m lower than it is today (Axelrod, 1966a). The forest retreated to higher, moister levels as the climate became drier, and the squirrels no doubt followed their food sources up into the mountains, and hence are not now in the lowlands of northern Baja California near closed-cone pines.

3. Another indication that squirrel and fire interaction may not have been a significant factor in the evolution of cone morphology is provided by a comparison of cones of the mainland and insular populations of P. remorata and P. muricata. There are no differences between the cones produced by pines on the Channel Islands and those on the mainland near Lompoc (Pine Canyon). There the pines are on dense chaparral-covered slopes, fires occur repeatedly, and squirrels are frequent. Clearly, the differences between the contrasting cone types in these pines must be due to other factors. As outlined earlier, remorata evidently is an ancient taxon. By contrast, muricata appears to be a relatively recent (probably post-glacial) hybrid, so its morphology can scarcely have been a response to continued fires and squirrel predation. One of its presumed near-parents (P. masonii Dorf) occurs in rocks as old as 9 m.y. and its cones have thick, sharply hooked apophyses like those of P. "borealis" from much younger rocks (compare Plates 12-16 with those of the present population, Plate 17). There was no significant change during this time, which is contrary to the postulate that fire-squirrel interaction has guided the evolution of cone morphology. If such a relation has existed, it must be ancient in this line of evolution.

Role of Mediterranean Climate

The trend to larger cones with larger seeds, more swollen apophyses, and greater asymmetry (see Plate 1) in the radiata pines may well repre-

sent an adaptation to increasing summer drought during the later Cenozoic.   Recall that the two taxa with the smallest cones, the smallest
seeds, the least swollen apophyses, and greatest symmetry are on Cedros
and Guadalupe islands, both areas with summer rainfall. Note also that
cones of the Cedros population are smaller than those of the Guadalupe
population, which is situated farther north toward California.   Both
islands have regular summer rain brought chiefly by the chubascos from
more southerly, subtropical latitudes. Note also that cones the size of
the Guadalupe population are recorded from the mainland in the Miocene
and Pliocene, when summer rainfall was present, and some persisted into
the Quaternary as well.

By contrast, the California populations with larger cones, larger and
more swollen apophyses heavier seeds, and greater asymmetry (Monterey →
Ano Nuevo → Cambria) inhabit areas of subhumid climate where precipitation is about 450 to 635 mm annually and summers are foggy. Since the
climatic trend of Miocene and later times involved a gradual decrease in
summer rainfall over California, the trend to larger cones with thicker
apophyses and larger seeds may have been a response to progressively
drier summers. In this regard, H.G. Baker (1972) has shown that there is
a relation between the weights of individual seeds and the environmental
conditions in which the plants that produce them live. For taxa whose
seedlings are exposed to the likelihood of drought following germination,
larger seeds would ensure more rapid root development, and hence survival
under the gradually increasing stress of longer periods of summer drought
in the emerging Mediterranean-type climate.

The sequence toward increased cone size, thicker apophyses, greater asymmetry, and larger, heavier seeds, which may reflect increasing summer drought over California during the later Cenozoic, seems consistent with the nature of the Cambria population. It inhabits an area dominated by open grassland and scattered clumps of live-oak woodland. Cambria has a drier climate than that where the Monterey and Ano Nuevo populations are adjacent to Pseudotsuga and Sequoia forests. The fact that the Cambria population does not have a known fossil record seems consistent with its presumed younger age, one corresponding with the emergence of a climate with a long period of drought (6 months with less than 2 mm) during the warm season.

On this basis, the occurrence of small-coned populations in the mountains of Cedros and Guadalupe islands seem expectable, for those areas receive more summer rain than California, and summer rain certainly was greater there in the Pliocene as well. Note also that the insular populations are nearer their inferred homeland in western Mexico, as outlined earlier. Furthermore, they have cones that more nearly approach the variation of Pinus oocarpa, which forms a possible prototype for evolution of the radiata group. Viewed in this manner, P. radiata cedrosensis, which does not now have a known fossil record, might well be judged a relict of Miocene and earlier times. At that time, Baja California was situated against the mainland (Sonora-Sinaloa-Jalisco) and Cedros Island was connected with the Sierra Viscaino to the southeast (Fig. 7). This would have provided a temperate upland climate suitable for invasion of the area from Mexico, an environment situated well above the lowlands that were dominated by arid tropic scrub and dry tropic forest (see Axelrod, 1979, fig. 15). Subsequent faulting and sea-floor spreading have isolated Cedros Island and Baja California from the mainland, and the California populations have been transported northward to a region where a very severe dry summer climate developed.

It is emphasized that while an increase in cone size, thicker apophyses, and larger seeds in radiata populations may be an adaptation to a progressively drier summer climate, it is not necessarily applicable to other "closed-cone pines." Cones of P. pretuberculata from the Miocene (12 m.y.) and Pliocene (7 m.y.) of California can scarcely be separated from those of the living attenuata, yet these Neogene records occur with taxa that clearly indicate adequate summer rain. Also, cones of P. masonii Dorf from the Pico Formation (age 9 m.y.) are thick and sharply hooked (Plate 12, figs. 1,2) and that pine also lived under adequate summer rainfall. Its close descendant, P. "borealis" Duffield, does not differ from it in any significant way. Note also that P. pungens Lamb from the rocky slopes of the middle Appalachian Mountains has cones with apophyses as thick and as prominently hooked as those of P. masonii, yet pungens lives under a climate of ample rain well distributed through the year, including a maximum in summer. Furthermore, recall that P. remorata Mason occurs in a very dry area southwest of San Vicente, Baja California, as does P. halepensis Miller along the north coast of Africa, yet both species have cone scales that are thin and and unarmed. Whereas P. remorata reaches down into the Pliocene, specimens similar to halepensis are recorded from Miocene and Oligocene rocks. Clearly, there have been diverse factors at work in shaping the morphology of pine cones over a period of millions of years.

Conclusion

The factors that account for the diversity of cone-scale morphology in the genus _Pinus_ are not known. It is important to realize that the major cone types of the principal subsections have considerable antiquity (Gaussen, 1960; Mirov, 1967). As noted previously, the Strobi go back into the Late Cretaceous; Cembroides are Middle Eocene; Balfourianae are in the Oligocene; the Ponderosae are Eocene; Contortae are Eocene; Sylvestres are Oligocene; and Sabinianae are Miocene. These are _minimum_ ages, based on fossil records that already represent these diverse groups: all of them must be older. The problem is compounded further by the coexistence of members of divergent subsections in the same fossil floras in Eocene time.

That the varied cone-scale morphology and degree of asymmetry shown by pine cones are the result of continued exposure to fire seems highly doubtful. That climate may at times have had a role in guiding morphologic change seems possible, as in the populations of _P. radiata_. But the coexistence, in the fossil record at the same site, of taxa representing members of divergent cone types of two or more subsections of the genus, militates against pinpointing climate as the overriding factor in their evolution. It is amply clear that _living animals_ have had little to do with the evolution of cone structure in _Pinus_ (or other conifers). That their antecedents may have been involved in the evolution of cone structure is possible, though such relationships reach so far back into the Tertiary they can scarcely be identified. Clearly, the present is not always the key to the past.

Extreme positions are of extreme value. They
induce the reader to think along different lines.
They break his conformist habits. (Feyerabend,
1970, p 111).

ACKNOWLEDGMENTS

During the course of this study, the staff of the herbaria at the University of California Berkeley; the California Academy of Sciences, San Francisco; the San Diego Museum of Natural History, and the Institute of Forest Genetics, U.S. Forest Service, Placerville, have been most cooperative in making available for study their extensive collections of modern closed-cone pines. Discussions with William B. Critchfield, Y. B. Linhart, G. Ledyard Stebbins, and Peter H. Raven have helped clarify several troublesome problems. An early draft of the manuscript was extensively criticized by Critchfield and Linhart. Although we disagree in some respects, their critical comments have been a great value in better formulating the history of the Californian Oocarpeae. Acknowledgment is also due Reid Moran for assistance in assembling the data in Tables 2 and 3. To all of them, my thanks.

This research has been greatly aided by a grant from the National Science Foundation which made it possible to visit Guadalupe and Cedros islands to see the southern populations of Monterey pine, and to examine mainland populations of closed-cone pines as well.

FOOTNOTES

1   This pine was named P. muricata var. cedrosensis Howell (1941, p. 7), but it shows no relation to muricata. The small trees are typically 2-needled, the cones are small (see Fig. 2) and ovate to slightly asymmetrical. The apophyses on the scales are not armed, but are typically rounded to slightly swollen. Examination of hundreds of cones on Cedros Island did not reveal the range of variation in cone-type displayed by muricata--from strongly asymmetric cones with strongly recurved, sharp apophyses, to those that are moderately asymmetric and with sharp but shorter apophyses, to those that approach P. remorata in symmetry and little or no armament. The small-coned Cedros Island pine is more nearly allied to P. radiata var. binata of Guadalupe Island than to the mainland forms of radiata. It is here renamed P. radiata var. cedrosensis (Howell).

2   The test is of the difference between means when variances are unknown and presumed unequal (Remington and Schork, 1970, p. 212). It assumes independent, random sampling from normally distributed populations.

3   Note that a comparison of Tables 2 and 3 readily demonstrates that the flora of Guadalupe, an oceanic island, is less rich than that of Cedros, a continental island.

4   Further study of variation in muricata cones suggests that in some areas (e.g., Purisima Hills, Pecho Hills) attenuata may also have been involved in its origin. If so, hybridization would have occurred under the influence of a moister climate than at present, either in immediate post-glacial time, or possibly in the Little Ice Age.

REFERENCES CITED

ABBOTT, P. L., and T. E. SMITH

    1978   Trace-element comparison of clasts in Eocene conglomerates, southwestern California and northwestern Mexico. Jour. Geology 86: 753-762.

AMUNDSON, D. C., and H. E. WRIGHT, JR.

    1979   Forest changes in Minnesota at the end of the Pleistocene. Ecol. Monogr. 40: 1-16.

ANDERSON, E., and G. L. STEBBINS, JR.

    1954   Hybridization as an evolutionary stimulus. Evolution 8: 378-388.

ARNOLD, C. A.

    1935   A Douglas fir cone from the Miocene of southeastern Oregon. Wash. Acad. Sci. Jour. 25: 378-380, fig. 1.

AXELROD, D. I.

    1937   A Pliocene flora from the Mount Eden beds, southern California. Carnegie Inst. Wash. Pub. 476: 125-183.

    1944   The Sonoma flora. In R. W. Chaney (ed.), Pliocene Floras of California and Oregon, Carnegie Inst. Wash. Pub. 553: 167-206.

1950   A Sonoma florule from Napa, California.   Carnegie Inst.
Wash. Pub. 590: 23-71.

1956   Mio-Pliocene floras from west-central Nevada.   Univ. Calif.
Pub. Geol. Sci. 33.   316 pp.

1958   Evolution of the Madro-Tertiary Geoflora.   Bot. Review 24:
433-509.

1966a   The Pleistocene Soboba flora of southern California.   Univ.
Calif. Pub. Geol. Sci. 60.   79 pp.

1966b   The Eocene Copper Basin flora of northeastern Nevada.   Univ.
Calif. Pub. Geol. Sci. 59.   83 pp.

1967a   Evolution of the California closed-cone pine forest.   In,
R. N. Philbrick (ed.), Proceedings of the Symposium on the
Biology of the California Islands, pp. 93-149.   Santa
Barbara Bot. Garden, Santa Barbara, Calif.

1967b   Geologic history of the California insular flora.   In, R. N.
Philbrick (ed.), Proceedings of the Symposium on the Biology
of the California Islands, pp. 267-315.   Santa Barbara Bot.
Garden, Santa Barbara, Calif.

1967c   Drought diastrophism and quantum evolution.   Evolution 21:
201-209.

1968   Tertiary floras and topographic history of the Snake River
basin, Idaho.   Geol. Soc. Amer. Bull. 79: 713-734.

1970   Mesozoic paleogeography and early angiosperm history.   Bot.
Review 36: 277-319.

1972   Edaphic aridity as a factor in angiosperm evolution.   Amer.
Naturalist 106: 311-320.

1975   Evolution and biogeography of Madrean-Tethyan sclerophyll
vegetation. Missouri Bot. Garden Ann. 62: 280-334.

1975   Evolution and biogeography of Madrean-Tethyan sclerophyll

        vegetation. Missouri Bot. Garden Ann. 62: 280-334.

1976a   History of the conifer forests, California and Nevada. Univ.

        Calif. Pub. Botany 70: 1-62.

1976b   Evolution of the Santa Lucia fir (<u>Abies</u> <u>bracteata</u>) ecosystem.

        Missouri Bot. Garden Ann. 63: 24-41.

1979   Age and origin of Sonoran Desert vegetation. Calif. Acad.

        Sci. Occas. Papers 132: 1-74.

BAILEY, H.P.

1964   Toward a unified concept of the temperate climate. Geogr.

        Review 54: 516-545.

BAKER, H. G.

1972   Seed weight in relation to environmental conditions in

        California. Ecology 53: 997-1110.

BAKER, O. E. (ed.)

1936   Atlas of American Agriculture--Physical Basis. U.S. Dept.

        Agric., Washington, D. C.

BANDY, O. L., and J. C. INGLE, JR.

1970   Neogene planktonic events and radiometric scale, California.

        Geol. Soc. Amer. Spec. Paper 124: 131-172.

BECK, M. E., JR., and P. W. PLUMLEY

1979   Late Cenozoic subduction and continental-margin truncation

        along the northern Middle America Trench: Discussion and

        reply (by D. E. Karig). Geol. Soc. Amer. Bull. 90: 792-794.

BERGER, R., and W. H. LIBBY

1966   UCLA radiocarbon dates. Radiocarbon 8: 467-497.

BLACK, C. C.

    1963   A review of the North American Tertiary Sciuridae. Bull.
            Mus. Compar. Zool., Harvard Univ., 130 (3): 113-248.

CAMPBELL, C. A

    1974   Paleoecological analysis of molluscan assemblages from the
            Pleistocene Millerton Formation. M.S. thesis, Univ. Cali-
            fornia, Davis. 114 pp.

CHANEY, R. W., and H. L. MASON

    1930   A Pleistocene flora from Santa Cruz Island, California.
            Carnegie Inst. Wash. Pub. 415: 1-24.

    1933   A Pleistocene flora from the asphalt deposits at Carpinteria,
            California. Carnegie Inst. Wash. Pub. 415: 45-79.

CRITCHFIELD, W. B.

    1957   Geographic variation in Pinus contorta. Maria Moors Chabot
            Found. Pub. 3. Cambridge, Mass.: Harvard Univ. Press. 118
            pp.

    1967   Crossability and relationships of the closed-cone pines.
            Silvae Genetica 16: 89-97.

    1972   Barriers to interbreeding within a single species--Pinus
            muricata. Abstract Western Forest Genetics Assoc., Corval-
            lis, Ore. Meeting, Aug. 2.

CRITCHFIELD, W. B., and E. L. LITTLE, JR.

    1966   Geographic distribution of the pines of the world. U.S.
            Dept. Agric., Forest Serv. Misc. Pub. 991. 97 pp.

CROWELL, J. C.

   1962   Displacement along the San Andreas fault, California.   Geol.

           Soc. Amer. Spec. Papers 71: 1-61.

   1975   San Andreas fault in southern California.   Calif. Div. Mines

           and Geol. Spec. Rept. 118.   272 pp.

DAUBENMIRE, R. F.

   1943   Vegetational zonation in the Rocky Mountains.   Bot. Rev. 9:

           325-393.

DIBBLEE, T. W., Jr.

   1966   Geology of the central Santa Ynez Mountains, Santa Barbara

           County, California.   Calif. Div. Mines and Geol. Bull. 186.

           99 pp.

DICKERSON, R. E.

   1922   Tertiary and Quaternary history of the Petaluma, Point Reyes,

           and Santa Rosa quadrangles, California.   Calif. Acad. Sci.

           Proc. 11: 527-601.

DORF, E.

   1930   Pliocene floras of California.   Carnegie Inst. Wash. Pub.

           412: 1-108.

DUFFIELD, J. W.

   1951   Interrelationships of the California closed-cone pines with

           special reference to _Pinus_ _muricata_ D. Don. Ph.D. thesis,

           Univ. California, Berkeley.   77 pp.

DURHAM, J. W.

   1954   The marine Cenozoic of southern California.   Calif. Div.

           Mines and Geol. Bull. 170, Chap. 3: 23-31.

DURHAM, J. W., R. H. JAHNS, and D. E. SAVAGE

    1954   Marine-nonmarine relationships in the Cenozoic section of
            California. Calif. Div. Mines and Geol. Bull. 170, Chap 3:
            59-71.

EASTWOOD, A.

    1929a   List of plants recorded from Cedros Island, Mexico. Proc.
            Calif. Acad. Sci. IV, 18: 420-441.

____ 1929b List of plants recorded from Guadalupe Island, Mexico. Prof.
            Calif. Acad. Sci. IV, 18: 394-420.

EHLERT, K. W., and P. L. EHLIG

    1977   The "polka-dot" granite and the rate of displacement of the
            San Andreas fault in southern California. Geol. Soc. Amer.,
            Abstracts with Programs 9 (4): 415-416.

EHLIG, P. L., K. W. EHLERT, and B. M. CROWE

    1975   Offset of the Upper Miocene Caliente and Mint Canyon forma-
            tions along the San Gabriel and San Andreas faults. Calif.
            Div. Mines and Geol. Spec. Rept. 118: 83-92.

EVERNDEN, J. F., and G. T. JAMES

    1964   Potassium-argon dates and the Tertiary floras of North
            America. Amer. Jour. Sci. 262: 945-974.

EVERNDEN, J. F., D. E. SAVAGE, G. H. CURTIS, and G. T. JAMES

    1964   Potassium-argon dates and the Cenozoic mammalian chronology
            of North America. Amer. Jour. Sci. 262: 145-198.

FERGUSSON, G. J., and W. F. LIBBY

    1964   UCLA Radiocarbon dates, III. Radiocarbon 6: 318-339.

FEYERABEND, P. K.

    1970   Against method: an outline of an anarchistic theory of
            knowledge. Univ. Minn. Studies in Philos. Sci. 4: 17-130.

FIELDING, J. M.

    1953   Variation in Monterey pine. For. Timb. Bur. Bull. 31: 1-43.

    1961   The pines of Cedros Island, Mexico. Australian Forestry 25:
             62-65.

FLINT, R.F.

    1971   Glacial and Quaternary Geology. New York: Wiley.   892 pp.

FLORIN, R.

    1951   Evolution in cordaites and conifers.   Acta Horti Bergiani
             15: 285-388.

FORDE, M. B.

    1964   Variation in natural populations of Pinus radiata in Cali-
             fornia, Part 3: Cone characters. New Zealand Jour. Bot. 2:
             459-485.

FROST, F. H.

    1927   The Pleistocene flora of Rancho La Brea.   Univ. Calif. Pub.
             Bot. 14: 73-98.

GALLOWAY, A. J.

    1977   Geology of the Point Reyes Peninsula, Marin Co., California.
             Calif. Div. Mines and Geol. Bull 190: 429-440.

GASTIL, R. G., R. P. PHILLIPS, and E. C. ALLISON

    1975   Reconnaissance Geology of the State of Baja California.
             Geol. Soc. Amer. Mem. 140. 170 p.

GASTIL, R. G., and W. JENSKY

    1973   Evidence for strike-slip displacement beneath the Trans-
             Mexican volcanic belt. Stanford Univ. Pub. Sci. 13: 181-190.

GASTIL, R.G., R. P. PHILLIPS, and R. RODRIGUEZ-TORRES

    1972   The reconstruction of Mesozoic California. 24th Internat.

            Geol. Congr., Montreal, Sec. 3: 217-229.

GAUSSEN, H.

    1960   Les gymnospermes actuelles et fossiles, tome 2, vol. 1, fasc.

            6, chap. 11: Generalites, Genre Pinus. Travaux du Labora-

            torie Forestier de Toulouse.

GEALEY, W. K.

    1951   Geology of the Healdsburg quadrangle, California. Calif.

            Div. Mines and Geol. Bull. 161: 1-50.

GLEN, W.

    1959   Pliocene and Lower Pleistocene of the western part of the

            San Francisco Peninsula. Univ. Calif. Pub. Geol. Sci. 36:

            147-198.

GRAHAM, S. A., and W. R. DICKINSON

    1978   Evidence for 115 kilometers of right slip on the San

            Gregorio-Hosgri fault trend. Science 199: 179-181.

GRIFFIN, J. R., and W. B. CRITCHFIELD

    1972   The distribution of forest trees in California. U. S.

            Department of Agriculture, Forest Service Research Paper

            PSW- 82/1972. 114 pp.

HOWELL, J. T.

    1941   The closed-cone pines of insular California. Leafl. West.

            Bot. 3: 1-8.

INGLE, J. C.

    1967   Foraminiferal biofacies variation and the Miocene-Pliocene

            boundary in southern California. Bulls. Amer. Paleontol. 52:

            217-394.

JENNINGS, C. W., and B. W. TROXEL

    1954   Ventura basin. Calif. Div. Mines and Geol. Bull. 170, Geol.

            Guide 2: 1-70.

JOHNSON, D. L.

    1977   The late Quaternary climate of coastal California: evidence

            for an Ice Age refugium. Quat. Research 8: 154-179.

JOHNSON, J. D., and W. R. NORMARK

    1974   Neogene tectonic evolution of the Salinian block, west-cen-

            tral California. Geology 2: 11-14.

KARIG, D. E., and W. JENSKY

    1972   The proto-Gulf of California. Earth and Planet. Sci. Let-

            ters 17: 169-174.

KILGORE, B.M., and D. TAYLOR

    1979   Fire history of a Sequoia-mixed conifer forest. Ecology 60:

            129-142.

KNOWLTON, F. H.

    1923   Fossil plants from the Tertiary lake beds of south-central

            Colorado. U. S. Geol. Surv. Prof. Paper 131-G: 183-197.

KOVACH, R. L., and A. NUR (eds.)

    1973   Proceedings of the conference on Tectonic problems of the

            San Andreas fault system. Stanford Univ. Pub. Geol. Sci.

            13. 494 pp.

LAWSON, A. C.

    1915   Geologic Atlas of the United States. San Francisco Folio,

            Folio no. 193: 1-180. U. S. Geol. Survey.

LINHART, Y. B.

    1978   Maintenance of variation in cone morphology in California

             closed-cone pines: the roles of fire, squirrels and seed

             output. Southwestern Naturalist 23: 29-40.

LINHART, Y. B., B. BURR, and M. T. CONKLE

    1967   The closed-cone pines of the northern Channel Islands. In

             R. B. Philbrick (ed.), Proceedings of the Symposium on the

             Biology of the California Islands, pp. 151-177.   Santa

             Barbara Botanic Garden, Santa Barbara, Calif.

LITTLE, E. L., JR., and W. B. CRITCHFIELD

    1969   Subdivisions of the Genus Pinus (Pines). U.S. Dept. Agric.,

             Forest Serv. Misc. Pub. 1144. 51 pp.

MACGINITIE, H. D.

    1953   Fossil plants of the Florissant Beds, Colorado. Carnegie

             Inst. Wash. Pub. 599. 188 pp.

    1969   The Eocene Green River flora of northwestern Colorado and

             northeastern Utah. Univ. Calif. Pub. Geol. Sci. 83. 140 p.

MARTIN, P. S., and J. GRAY

    1962   Pollen analysis and the Cenozoic. Science 137: 103-111.

MARTINEZ, MAXIMINO.

    1948   Los Pinos Mexicanos, 2nd ed. Mexico City: Ediciones Botas.

MASON, H. L.

    1927   Fossil records of some west American conifers. Carnegie

             Inst. Wash. Pub. 346: 139-158.

    1930   The Santa Cruz Island Pine. Madroño 2: 8-10.

    1932   A phylogenetic series of the California closed-cone pines

             suggested by the fossil record. Madroño 2(6): 49-55.

1934   Pleistocene flora of the Tomales Formation. Carnegie Inst.
          Wash. Pub. 415: 81-179.

1949   Evidence for the genetic submergence of Pinus remorata. In
          G. L. Jepsen, G. G. Simpson, and E. Mayr (eds.), Genetics,
          Paleontology and Evolution, Pp. 356-362. Princeton, N.J.:
          Princeton Univ. Press.

MATTHEWS, V., III

1976   Correlation of Pinnacles and Neenach volcanic formations and
          their bearing on the San Andreas fault problem. Amer.
          Assoc. Petrol. Geol. Bull. 60: 2128-2141.

MILLER, C. N., JR.

1976   Early evolution in the Pinaceae. Rev. Paleobot. Palynol.
          21: 101-117.

1977   Mesozoic conifers. Bot. Review 43: 217-280.

MIROV, N. T.

1967   The genus Pinus. New York: Ronald Press. 602 pp.

MOORE, D. G.

1973   Plate-edge deformation and crustal growth, Gulf of Califor-
          nia structural province. Geol. Soc. Amer. Bull. 84: 1883-
          1906.

MOORE, J. C.

1959   Relationships among living squirrels of the Sciurinae. Bull.
          Amer. Mus. Nat. Hist. 118 (4): 153-206.

1961   The spread of existing diurnal squirrels across the Bering
          and Panamanian land bridges. Amer. Mus. Novitates 2044:
          1-26.

NEWCOMB, G. B.

   1962   Geographic variation in _Pinus attenuata_ Lemmon.   Ph.D.
            thesis, Univ. California, Berkeley.   191 p.

PUTNAM, W. C.

   1942   Geomorphology of the Ventura region, California.   Geol. Soc.
            Amer. Bull. 53: 691-754.

RAVEN, P. H., and D. I. AXELROD

   1977   Origin and relationships of the California flora.   Univ.
            Calif. Pub. Botany 72: 1-134.

REMINGTON, R. D., and M. A. SCHORK

   1970   Statistics with applications to the biological and health
            sciences.   Englewood Cliffs, N.J.:   Prentice Hall.   418 pp.

RICHARDS, H. G., and D. L. THURBER

   1966   Pleistocene age determinations from California and Oregon.
            Science 152: 1091-1092.

SEIDERS, V. M.

   1978   Onshore stratigraphic comparisons across the San Simeon and
            Hosgri faults, California.   Geol. Soc. Amer. 74th Ann. Mtg.,
            Abstracts with Programs 10 (3): 146.

SHAW, G. R.

   1914   The genus _Pinus_.   Arnold Arb. Pub. 5.   96 p.   Harvard Univ.

SILVER, E. A., AND W. R. NORMARK (eds.)

   1978   San Gregorio-Hosgri fault zone, Calif.   Calif. Div. Mines
            and Geol. Spec. Report 137.   56 pp.

SIMPSON, G. G.

   1953   The Major Features of Evolution. New York: Columbia Univ.
            Press.   434 pp.

SMITH, A. G.

   1976   Plate tectonics and orogeny: a review. Tectonophysics 33:

            215-285.

SMITH, C. C.

   1970   The coevolution of pine squirrels (<u>Tamiasciurus</u>) and coni-

            fers. Ecol. Monogr. 40: 350-371.

SMITH, D. P.

   1977   San Juan-St. Francis Fault--hypothesized major middle Ter-

            tiary right-lateral fault in central and southern Califor-

            nia. Calif. Div. Mines and Geol. Spec. Rept. 129: 41-50.

STEBBINS, G. L.

   1952   Aridity as a stimulus to plant evolution. Amer. Naturalist

            86: 33-44.

   1974   Flowering Plants: Evolution above the Species Level. Cam-

            bridge, Mass.: Belknap Press (Harvard). 399 pp.

STEBBINS, G. L., and J. MAJOR

   1965   Endemism and speciation in the California flora. Ecol.

            Monogr. 35: 1-35.

TRAVIS, R. B.

   1952   Geology of the Sebastopol Quadrangle, California. Calif.

            Div. Mines and Geol. Bull. 162: 1-33.

WEAVER, C. E.

   1949   Geology of the Coast Ranges immediately north of the San

            Francisco Bay region, California. Geol. Soc. Amer. Memoir

            35: 1-242.

WILSON, A. C., S. S. CARLSON, and T. J. WHITE

   1977   Biochemical evolution. Ann. Rev. Biochem. 46: 573-639.

WOLFE, J.

    1964   Miocene floras from Fingerrock Wash, southwestern Nevada. U. S. Geol. Surv. Prof. Paper 454-N. 36 pp.

WOODRING, W. R., M. N. BRAMLETTE, and W. S. W. KEW

    1946   Geology and paleontology of Palos Verdes Hills, California. U. S. Geol. Surv. Prof. Paper 207. 145 pp.

YEATS, R. S. and W. A. MCLAUGHLIN

    1970   Potassium-argon mineral age of an ash bed in the Pico Formation, Ventura Basin, California. Geol. Soc. Spec. Paper 124: 173-206.

ZAVARIN, E., K. SNAJBERK, and J. FISHER

    1975   Geographic variability of monoterpens from cortex of _Abies concolor_. Biochem. Systematics and Ecol. 3: 191-203.

PLATES

All figures are shown at natural size.

The collections are deposited in the Museum
of Paleontology, University of California,
Berkeley, [unless otherwise noted.]

PLATE 1

Mean cone size of Monterey pine populations as depicted in text
figure 2. The populations are (1) Cedros Island, (2) Guadalupe Island,
(3) Monterey, (4) Ano Nuevo, and (5) Cambria.

PLATE 2

Pinus radiata D. Don. Millerton. Hypotype nos. 5762-5766.

PLATE 3

Pinus radiata D. Don.   Millerton.   Hypotype nos. 5767-5770.

PLATE 4

Pinus radiata D. Don.   Near Pt. Sal.   Hypotype nos. 5787-5788.

PLATE 5

Pinus radiata D. Don.   Near Pt. Sal.   Hypotype nos. 5789-5791.

PLATE 6

Pinus radiata D. Don. Veronica Springs Quarry. Santa Barbara Museum of Natural History, Hypotype no. 473. This cluster of 4 cones is preserved in a concretion.

PLATE 7

Pinus radiata D. Don.   Veronica Springs Quarry.   Santa Barbara
Museum of Natural History.   Figs. 1-3, Hypotype nos. 476-478.   Fig. 4 is
a latex cast of cone impression, Hypotype no. 475.

PLATE 8

Pinus lawsoniana Axelrod.   Drakes Bay.   Hypotype nos. 5799, 5800.

PLATE 9

Pinus lawsoniana Axelrod.   Drakes Bay.   Hypotype nos. 5801, 5802.

PLATE 10

Pinus lawsoniana Axelrod.   Drakes Bay.   Hypotype nos. 5803-5806.

PLATE 11

Pinus muricata D. Don. Cones from the population on the crest of La

Purisima Hills north of Lompoc, adjacent to State Highway 1. This is

typical of the variation of the taxon termed var. typica by Duffield.

Note that the variation ranges from strongly asymmetrical cones with

pronounced hooks on the cone scales to symmetrical cones with smooth and

thin scales.

PLATE 12

Figs. 1, 2. *Pinus* *masonii* Dorf. Lower Pico. Cotype nos. 306, 307. Previously figured by Dorf (1930).

Figs. 3, 4. *Pinus* *masonii* Dorf. Lower Merced. Hypotype nos. 159, 20532. Previously figured by Dorf (1930) and Axelrod (1967a), respectively.

PLATE 13

Pinus "borealis" Duffield.   Carpinteria.   Hypotype nos. 5924-5929.

PLATE 14

Pinus "borealis" Duffield.   Carpinteria.   Santa Barbara Museum of Natural History.   Hypotype nos. 467-472.

PLATE 15

Pinus "borealis" Duffield.   Near Pt. Sal.   Hypotype nos. 5844-5849.

PLATE 16

Pinus "borealis" Duffield.   Near Pt. Sal.   Hypotype nos. 5850-5855.

PLATE 17

Cones of the living Pinus "borealis" Duffield from groves near Timber Cove, Sonoma Co., California. This taxon, previously considered to represent P. muricata D. Don, has cones that differ markedly from those of muricata (see Plates 11 and 20).

PLATE 18

Cones of _Pinus_ _remorata_ Mason from a gove southwest of San Vicente, Baja California.   The trees are 4.8 km (3 mi.) by road south of Cerro Colorado, which is on the coast west of San Vicente.   The grove is on the second terrace, in the entrenched meanders of the creek that flows seaward from Canon de los Pinitos, and at an elevation of about 100 m.

PLATE 19

Figs. 1, 4. *Pinus remorata* Mason. Century City, Hypotype nos. 5841, 5840.

Fig. 2. *Pinus remorata* Mason. Santa Cruz Island. Hypotype no. 5839.

Fig. 3. *Pinus remorata* Mason. Near Pt. Sal. Hypotype no. 5840.

Fig. 5. *Pinus remorata* Mason. Carpinteria. Santa Barbara Museum of Natural History, Hypotype no. 474.

PLATE 20

Cones from populations of <u>Pinus</u> <u>remorata</u> Mason, <u>P</u>. <u>muricata</u> D. Don (var. "<u>typica</u>" Duffield), and <u>P</u>. "<u>borealis</u>" Duffield. It is apparent that <u>P</u>. <u>muricata</u> seems to be a hybrid, and evidently is of Late Wisconsin or post-glacial age. No fossil suites are yet known that display the variation of <u>Pinus</u> <u>muricata</u> var. "<u>typica</u>."

REMORATA   MURICATA   "BOREALIS"